From SERVANTHOOD To SONSHIP

A Roadmap To Servant Leadership

Jesse A. McCrary

From SERVANTHOOD To SONSHIP
A Roadmap To Servant Leadership

Jesse A. McCrary

© 2020 Divine Works Publishing

From **Servanthood** *To* **Sonship**

ALL RIGHTS RESERVED. No part of this publication may be reproduced, stored in a retrieval system, or transmitted in any form or by any means, electronic, mechanical, photocopying, recording or otherwise without the prior permission of the publisher or in accordance with the provisions of the Copyright, Designs, and Patents Act 1988 or under the terms of any license permitting limited copying issued by the Copyright Licensing Agency.

Scripture Quotations are from the King James Version of the Bible, except where otherwise noted.

The views expressed in this work are solely those of the author and do not necessarily reflect the views of the publisher, the publisher hereby disclaims any responsibility for them.

ISBN-13: 978-1-949105-12-4 (paperback)
ISBN-13: 978-1-949105-29-2 (eBook)

For Worldwide Distribution, Printed in the U.S.A

Published by:
Divine Works Publishing, LLC
Royal Palm Beach, Florida USA

www.DivineWorksPublishing.com
561-990-BOOK (2665)

Dedication:

To God,

I am still ever amazed at how you choose to use me in the capacity that you do. I am overwhelmed by the unwavering love that you constantly shed upon me and I am ever so grateful for that. I look forward to what and how you are going to use me in this season. Thank you, does not seem to be enough so I willingly give back to you what you have freely given to me in order to bless your people.

Table of Contents

Acknowledgments | ix
Foreword | xi

Part I

Chapter 1   *The Ministry of Help* | 1

Chapter 2   *As Unto the Lord* | 9

Chapter 3   *Y'all Don't Hear Me:*
                 The Accounts of Miriam and Aaron | 17

Chapter 4   *Glutton for Punishment:*
                 The Accounts of the Children of Israel | 23

Chapter 5   *Friend or Foe:*
                 The Accounts of Korah | 29

Chapter 6   *Integrity Issues* | 33

Chapter 7   *A Cancerous Cell?* | 39

Part II

Chapter 8   *Captivated Heart* | 47

Chapter 9   *The Role of Spiritual Fathers* | 53

Chapter 10   *The Father's Expectation* | 63

Chapter 11   *Finding Your Fit* | 69

Chapter 12   *Final Words* | 83

Acknowledgments

To my daughter Charis Alethia, thank you for your love and for always seeing daddy as no one else sees me. Always know that you are my heart's joy and not only the apple of God's eye, but my eye too. I know that God has great plans for you as well and I am looking forward to seeing God manifesting His power and purpose through your life.

To Felicia, thank you for being such an awesome mother and that constant support for our daughter.

To my pop, my mentor, spiritual father, my Elijah, Dr. Bennett Smith, you have always had my best interests at heart and for that I am truly grateful. I look forward to what God has in store for us as we walk out his plan for our lives.

To my pastor, Bishop Henry Fernandez, words cannot begin to express how grateful I am for the opportunity that you have afforded me. What you have done in the life of my family and I cannot be summarized in this short statement, but know that I am truly thankful that God has placed you in our lives for such a time as this.

To Pastor Iran Pitre, Thank you for your contribution to this book. It was a great honor to have your insight regarding "Finding Your Fit."

To my publisher, I don't know how to thank you for all that you have done. From the moment that I shared the heart of my book, you ran with it until the end. Thank you for your insight and for all that you have done to help launch my book.

I look forward with great expectation to what God has in store as we continue to work together.

To my mom, Margaret E. McCrary, my educator, disciplinarian, supporter, the quiet force constantly pushing me in my back to go farther than I thought I could. I know I don't say it enough but I am truly thankful to you and love you so very much.

Lastly, to my dad, Earl Phillip McCrary, the one who lived to serve others. You have taught me the most on what it means to serve others and how to serve with a pure heart and pure motives...know that I love and miss you. Although you are not here to physically witness the birth of my first book...know that this one's for you.

Foreword

When you consider the words of Jesus in Matthew 20, it's easy to understand why He places such high importance on the subject of servanthood. In verses 27 and 28, Jesus said: "And whoever desires to be first among you, let him be your slave—just as the Son of Man did not come to be served, but to serve, and to give His life a ransom for many."

Jesus was, and is the only begotten Son of God. Yet, as the Savior of the world, He willingly laid aside His exalted position as King of kings and Lord of lords and became the true and living example of what God desires that we all be—servants! Why? Because servant hood, faithfully executed from the heart, is representative of true sonship. It reflects the character of God, His Son, and His love for all mankind.

Nowhere is the subject of servanthood more prevalent, and its demonstration more revealing than in the lives of Jesus, and other prominent Bible characters. In this thought-provoking book, Jesse McCrary journeys through the scriptures and draws from some of those stories as he examines what it truly means to be a servant, and how serving transitions us into a Sonship relationship with our heavenly Father. He explores the lives of people who were hand-picked by God—people whose selfless lifestyles reflected love, compassion and hearts to serve.

Having a sonship relationship with God is something every believer should desire. But as His representatives on the earth, it's important to recognize that sonship and service go together. Service to others should always be the order of the day—our lifestyle of choice. It's one of the ways we can best represent

Christ to the world. It also confirms that we are God's sons and daughters.

Read this book, then examine yourself. Decide if you're on the path that every Christian should be traveling—the path that leads to a true relationship with your heavenly Father. Do you see yourself as a child of God whose desire is to be served? Or, have you entered His Sonship because, like Jesus, you have a strong willingness to be a servant to others?

—Henry Fernandez

Senior Pastor, The Faith Center
Fort Lauderdale, Florida

Chapter 1

The Ministry of Help

"And God hath set some in the church. first apostles, secondarily prophets, thirdly teachers, after that miracles, then gifts of healing, Help, governments, diversities of tongues." –1 Corinthians 12:28

Several years ago while at a church in Louisiana, I was asked to enter the main sanctuary. As I walked into the sanctuary, I was called up to the front and the pastor used me as an example to show how angels go with and stand by us. As I was leaving the sanctuary that particular night, one of the ministers said, "Everything changes for you from this night forward". I cannot tell you how right he was. I made a commitment to serve my pastor directly even if that meant being at the church earlier and staying later—I just did it. If he needed me to drive him in town or out of town, I did it. If there was a need for me to type up some information for him or research some information for him, I did it. More importantly than all of those things, I made the commitment to undergird him in prayer so that he would be able to stand and effectively minister the Word of God.

As time progressed, the Lord began to deal with me in the

area of servanthood and what it meant, not just to be a servant who acted as a son, but what it meant to be a son who willingly served.

As the years passed, God increased my wisdom and understanding of the Ministry of Help. I began to look more closely at this ministry and the significant impact that it has on the body of Christ as a whole. So, as I begin to discuss in much greater depth the overall Ministry of Help, First, it is necessary to put into perspective the context in which the twelfth chapter of Corinthians was written. The Corinthian people were once pagan worshipers who were converted to Christianity. Paul addressed some critical issues pertaining to the area of spiritual gifts—as some regarded themselves better than others based on their gifting. Paul strongly wanted them not to think themselves more highly than what they should and understand that each gift was necessary for the body of Christ (The Church) to function as a complete unit.

While we yet can see the great diversities of gifts that the Lord bestowed upon the church at Corinth, we also see the great controversy that was stirred up, because of how they esteemed themselves over one another. In his response, Paul takes the opportunity to clearly explain:

- There are diversities of gifts.
- The gifts are given by the same Lord.
- The same God works in all.
- The gifts are meant to profit all.
- The Lord decides to whom what gifts are given.

Let's take a closer look at the Corinthian Church. There was much arrogance and pride among the Corinthians. All too often we find pride to be a common problem in the body of Christ today. Essentially, we ought to pay close attention to what Paul stated:

"REMEMBER how you were when you didn't know God, led from one phony god to another, never knowing what you were doing, just doing it because everybody else did it? It's different in this life. God wants us to use our intelligence, to seek and understand as well as we can."

1 Corinthians 12:1-3 says: (The Message Bible)

"What I want to talk about now is the various ways God's Spirit gets worked into our lives. This is complex and often misunderstood, but I want you to be informed and knowledgeable. Remember how you were when you didn't know God, led from one phony god to another, never knowing what you were doing, just doing it because everybody else did it? It's different in this life."

Paul simply says, listen brethren don't get beside yourself in regards to the spiritual gifts that have been bestowed upon you. It was not too long ago that you were once lost and ignorant to the things of God yourself and just followed the crowd. I want you to consider some other passages of scripture that Paul wrote in regards to not being consumed with ourselves.

Ephesians 2:11-12 says:

"Wherefore remember, that ye being in time past Gentiles in the flesh, who are called Uncircumcision by that which is called the Circumcision in the flesh made by hands; That at that time ye were without Christ, being aliens from the commonwealth of Israel, and strangers from the covenants of promise, having no hope, and without God in the world..."

Titus 3:3 says:

"For we ourselves also were sometimes foolish, disobedient, deceived, serving divers lusts and pleasures, living in malice and envy, hateful, and hating one another."

1 Peter 5:5 says:

"*Likewise, ye younger, submit yourselves unto the elder. Yea, all of you be subject one to another, and be clothed with humility: for God resisteth the proud, and giveth grace to the humble. Humble yourselves therefore under the mighty hand of God, that he may exalt you in due time...*"

In the few passages of scripture presented, you can clearly see that it is to no benefit to elevate oneself up on a pedestal. You must understand that every part in the body of Christ is significant to the overall function of the church. While there are many passages of scripture we can pull out, I want to be sure that you have a good understanding in regards to the Ministry of Help.

Sons and Servants

Let's look closely at the Ministry of Help (servanthood) so that there is no confusion as to the effectiveness of this ministry. As I said earlier, God began to instruct me in the aspect of servanthood and what it meant to be a son who serves as opposed to a servant who acts as a son. Now just for clarity sake, I want you to understand that there is a distinct difference between a servant and a son/daughter and this is what God wanted to do in my life. He wanted to bring me from the aspect of a servant playing the role of a son to a son who willingly and unselfishly serves.

Hebrews 3:5-6 deals with the perspective of Moses and Christ. "*And Moses verily was faithful in all his house, as a servant, for a testimony of those things which were to be spoken after; But Christ as a son over his own house; whose house are we, if we hold fast the confidence and the rejoicing of the hope firm unto the end.*"

In this passage of scripture that the writer of Hebrews stated that Moses was a faithful servant in His (God's) house as opposed to Jesus Christ being a faithful son over His (God's) house.

When we speak of the "house," of course we are speaking of the House of God. So Moses operated in a servant capacity in the House of God while Christ operated as the Son in the House of God. Servants do as they are told to do and operate in very little authority as Moses did. A son walks in and operates under the authority given by the Father.

Consider this passage of scripture found in Ephesians 2:6. *"And hath raised us up together, and made us sit together in heavenly places in Christ Jesus..."*

The key word I want to point out in this passage of scripture is the word *"in."* We are seated together in heavenly places "IN" Christ Jesus. This is very different from sitting "with" Christ. If we are seated "IN" Christ and Christ is "IN" us, then we ultimately share or partake in the authority He has as well. Romans 8:14-17 clearly addresses those that are led by the Spirit as sons and sons/daughters walk and operate in the authority given by their father.

"For as many as are led by the Spirit of God, they are the sons of God. For ye have not received the spirit of bondage again to fear; but ye have received the Spirit of adoption, whereby we cry, Abba, Father. The Spirit itself beareth witness with our spirit, that we are the children of God: And if children, then heirs; heirs of God, and joint-heirs with Christ; if so be that we suffer with him, that we may be also glorified together."

Help Me

The word help means to "aid, assist, help;" or those who render aid, assistance, or help; helpers. The Bible does not clearly state who these particular people were; however, they could have been anyone. They may have been anyone entrusted to care for the poor, the sick, strangers, orphans, widows, homeless and/or they could have been those functioning in the office of deacons or perhaps even laymen. They could have even been those who attended to the apostles to aid them in their *"work"* such as those to whom Paul referred to in Romans 16:3 (King James) *"Greet Priscilla and Aquila my helpers in Christ Jesus."*

The Bible is full of examples of how the body of Christ should function as one complete unit working together for the overall common goal, which is Christ. The Apostle Paul wrote in 1 Corinthians 12:14-22 how the body should function. Paul states that one part of the body cannot say it has no need of another part saying that I wish I were this part. Let's say that God granted the ear to be an eye...you know the ear would not be turned into an eye, it would just be an ear in the place of the eye. How crazy would that look? In essence, it is of great importance that we honor the place where God has put us by staying there and doing our part. I want us to look at one other passage of scripture found in Ephesians 4:16. Once the body functions as a complete unit, working together for a common goal, it is then that we will see rapid mature growth in the body.

If the body of Christ is going to be effective in what she is called to do, it is time that we firmly take our position, be it great or small. There have been enough *"casualties of war"* falling to the wayside of people who have been hurt, overlooked, or ran off and we don't need any more. We cannot function to our full potential when there is disharmony among the body. (Luke 11:17 Amplified)

> *"But He, [well aware of their intent and purpose, said to them, Every kingdom split up against itself is doomed and brought to desolation, and so house falls upon house. [The disunited household will elapse.]"* (Matthew 12:25 Amplified.)

We cannot be victorious in the battle against our enemy if we are warring internally. It is imperative that we begin to deal with the enemy in a "Me" mindset. Often times, the biggest enemy we face is the one within us. So many times people have difficulty getting past their own insecurities that it greatly hinders them from achieving all that God has for them. As a part of the body of Christ, it is time that we deal with the issues we have within ourselves by first dealing with our own so that we are placed in a position whereby we are helping and not hurting one another. Do you remember the incident in Luke 9:49-50?

"And John answered and said, Master, we saw one casting out devils in thy name; and we forbade him, because he followeth not with us. And Jesus said unto him, Forbid him not: for he that is not against us is for us."

The disciples basically decided that since this man who was casting out devils was not a part of their clique or club; that they were going to stop him from doing the work of the Lord. How arrogant and selfish was that on the part of the disciples? Here it is that they went around teaching and preaching the Message of the gospel, yet when they see someone whom they did not know doing the same thing that they were teaching the people, they had a problem with them, and tried to stop them. It sounds much like situations we deal with today. As long as we are doing what some require then we're OK, but no sooner than we start making progress... "Who does she think she is; he must think he is all that." I thought we were all working for the common good to *"preach Christ and Him crucified."* (1 Corinthians 1:23)

> 1 Corinthians 12:27 says, *"Now ye are the body of Christ, and members in particular."*

There is a particular grace upon our lives to operate in the gifts and callings that God has placed in each of us; therefore, all members of the body are significant to the overall functioning. I believe that Ephesians 4:16 says it best.

"From whom the whole body fitly joined together and compacted by that which every joint supplieth, according to the effectual working in the measure of every part, maketh increase of the body unto the edifying of itself in love."

Chapter 2

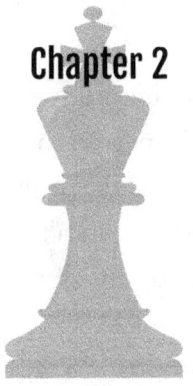

As Unto The Lord

"And whatsoever you do in word or deed, do all in the name of the Lord Jesus, giving thanks to God and the Father by him."
(Colossians 3:17)

"Whether therefore you eat, or drink, or whatsoever you do, do all to the glory of God."
(1 Corinthians 10:31)

Check Your Motives

While serving at a ministry in Louisiana, I was asked one day by the administrator to cut the grass in front of the church. I will not dive into the details of how big this piece of land is, but trust me it is big. I must admit that pride and arrogance rose up in me and I said within myself, "I don't cut grass, that is not what I am called to do." How quickly the Lord rebuked me on that issue I cannot even tell you, but from that day on I looked forward to cutting the grass at the church.

Allow me to ask you a few questions servants. How well do you scrub toilets? How well do you pick up trash around the church where you are located? How well do you serve others? I am not just talking about those with whom you agree, but the ones that you don't. How well do you serve your Man or Women of God even when you don't agree with what they are doing? A true servant must have a deep-down sense of respect for their leaders and acceptance of him/her, tolerance of the leaders' personalities, and their way of doing things. If you are in a position of serving your pastor and you can't seem to follow his or her orders, then you may want to check your motives, more importantly your level of submission to God. You may say what does being submitted to God have to do with my being submitted to my pastor? I am glad you asked. The Word of God says:

"Servants, do what you're told by your earthly masters. And don't just do the minimum that will get you by. Do your best. Work from the heart for your real Master, for God, confident that you'll get paid in full when you come into your inheritance. Keep in mind always that the ultimate Master you're serving is Christ. The sullen servant who does shoddy work will be held responsible. Being Christian doesn't cover up bad work." (Colossians 3:22-25)

Carry Their Heart

While it is natural for us to want some type of accolade, please understand that, this is not the goal of servanthood. The ultimate goal in all things, not just servanthood, is to please God. What we must understand is that when we are obedient to those to who we're in submission to, we are then obeying God. Our position and mind-set should always be to help advance the vision that God has given our pastors, not slow it down or hinder it. In other words, we must always be in a position to do whatever is in their hearts. Let's consider the scene of Jonathan and his armour bearer:

"And Jonathan said to the one that bare his armour, Come,

and let us go over unto the garrison of these uncircumcised; It may be that the Lord will work for us: for there is no restraint to the Lord to save by many or by few. And his armour bearer said unto him, Do all that is in thine heart: turn thee; behold, I am with thee according to thy heart." (1 Samuel 14:6-7)

This passage of scripture is rather interesting to me simply because of the statement Jonathan makes to his armour bearer. Here Jonathan says "IT MAY BE..." It gives the impression that he is not really sure, but we'll just try this to see what happens. More surprising but very important is the response that his armour bearer gives him. He says "DO ALL that is in thine HEART...behold, I am with you according to thy HEART." We can see here that not only did Jonathan's armour bearer learn to carry his amour, but most of all, he also learned how to carry his heart.

My God!!! It is so important servants that we learn to carry the hearts of the ones that we are serving. So many times pastors lose out because those they have trusted are the same ones that turn their backs on them. It is obvious that there was great sense of trust on the part of Jonathan's servant seeing how he was willing to go even in the midst of what seem to be uncertainty on Jonathan's part. Moreover, he trusted Jonathan with his life completely. There cannot be a one-sided trust factor; both the pastor and servant must be able to trust one another.

So there they were the two of them and Jonathan is the only one who carried a sword. He instructed his armour bearer that "if they say we will come to you, then we will stay in our place. But if they say you come up to us then we will go because the Lord has delivered them into the hands of Israel". Keep in mind that Jonathan is still the only one with a sword. As they revealed themselves to the garrison of the Philistines, one of the soldiers in the Philistine army beckoned "Come up to us and we will show you a thing." Jonathan commanded his armour bearer "let's go!" and climbed upon his hands with his armour bearer steady after him. Jonathan struck the first one down and his armour bearer slayed after him. You may ask what happened. I thought Jonathan was the only one with a sword? Yes, initially Jonathan was the only one, but after he incited the first kill, his armour bearer picked up a sword and slew after him. This is a very important passage of scripture because it is indicative of the character and attitude that we as servants should have when it comes to serving the people God has called us to serve. Too many times we allow our pastors or leaders to go into battle alone and thus risk utter defeat and humiliation. This should not be the case; we should always be ever so ready to go to war with and/or on behalf of our Men and Women of God.

Is He Worth Risking Your Life For?

Consider the men that were serving King David and what they said to him concerning what would be his last battle:

One day David had grown weary when he and his soldiers were fighting the Philistines and one of the Philistine warriors was Ishbibenob, who was a descendant of the Rephaim, and he tried to kill David. Ishbibenob was armed with a new sword and his bronze spearhead alone weighed seven and a half pounds.

"But Abishai came to the rescue and killed the Philistine. David's soldiers told him, "We can't let you risk your life in battle anymore! You give light to our nation, and we want that flame to keep burning." (2 Samuel 21:17)

David's men told him that he was important to the kingdom; that he was the light of Israel and they could not afford to lose him. How important is your pastor or leader to you, servant? How far are you willing to go in order to help preserve them?

Are you weak and timid in nature? If so, do yourself and your pastor a world of good and take some time to develop yourself. There is no room for jellyfish when it comes to serving in the Kingdom of God. Notice how David's men were willing to risk their lives for him in order to bring him a drink.

Now, I want to look more closely at the life of David as expressed in 1 Samuel, chapter 16. To not include an excessive amount of scripture, I will paraphrase the story for you.

We find David, who is a Shepherd boy, tending to his father's sheep. The Prophet Samuel visits David's father—Jesse's house— in order to anoint a new king in Saul's stead. Jesse parades all of his sons in front of Samuel except for David. The Prophet asked if there was another son and Jesse replies yes, but that he is just a shepherd boy. Samuel told Jesse to bring the boy and he would not sit down until he came . So Jesse sent for David, Samuel got a witness from the Lord, and he anoints David as king. As the story goes David ended up playing the harp for King Saul because an evil spirit from the Lord would come upon him and David's harp playing relieved the king.

We also discover that after David returns from the slaughter of the Philistines that the women from all the cities of Israel come out to meet King Saul with musical instruments and dancing. They begin to sing to one another, "Saul has slain his thousand and David his ten thousands" thus beginning Saul's jealousy and hatred for David for he said, "They have given David ten thousands, and to me they have given only thousands. And what more can he have but the kingdom? And Saul eyed David from that day and forward." Here David was only doing what was required of him and Saul became jealous and began to hate the very one he loved greatly and that had found favour in his sight.

I am very sure that it must have been a very difficult time for David serving someone that was out to kill him. Now I want you to pay close attention because if that were any of us, we would have been gone at the first javelin. Please understand servants, I know that it gets hard sometimes and it seems as if things are sometimes unbearable, but believe me if you conduct yourself as David did you will see the salvation of the Lord. The Bible says that David avoided Saul's presence twice. David also gives us a very clear reflection on how we should respond to our pastors or leaders even in a life-threatening situation:

"And David behaved himself wisely in all his ways; and the Lord was with him"

Now can we honestly say that we would conduct ourselves like David did? If your answer is no, then I would suggest that you ask yourself who am I serving man or God? I am in no ways trying to make an excuse for Saul in regards to his actions. Neither am I trying to make an excuse for those pastors who treat their servants badly; however, I believe it is very pertinent that we take on the attitude that David had as it related to his "pastor" Saul. How many times have servants become victims of coercion and end up doing something that they had no business doing? Let's consider what David's men said to him in regards to Saul:

"And the men of David said to him, Behold, this is the day of which Jehovah said to you, Behold, I will deliver your enemy into your hand so that you may do to him as it shall seem good to you. And David arose and cut off the skirt of Saul's robe secretly.

And it happened afterward that David's heart struck him because he had cut off Saul's skirt. And he said to his men, far be it from me, by Jehovah, if I will do this thing to my lord, Jehovah's anointed, to stretch forth my hand against him, since he is the anointed of Jehovah." (1 Samuel 24:4-6)

In this chapter David fled to the mountains with his men in order to escape from the hands of Saul. It came to pass that Saul took rest in a cave and David's men basically say that it was the Prophecy of God coming to pass, now go and avenge yourself. Allow me to say this as a side note...We need to be careful of who you allow to speak into our ears in regarding what the Lord is saying in this present hour. It sounds as if David's men wanted more revenge then what he wanted. Servants, be careful of what you say to your man or woman of God, it just may cost them. David cuts off the skirt of Saul's robe secretly and right after he is grieved for doing such a thing. While David may have had a very valid reason to avenge himself for what Saul was trying to do to him, I believe that the more important thing to take note of here is that David recognized to whom he was ultimately submitted.

It is also interesting to note that David knew he was to be king. The prophet Samuel came to his father's house and anointed him to be king in Saul's stead. So, David knew he was the next king; however, regardless of that truth, David still regarded Saul as the Lord's anointed. How do you regard your pastor in the midst of adversity? Do you take on the same mindset as David, or do you take matters into your own hands? Here is the ultimate question, even during adversity with your pastor; can you still stay submitted and committed? I am not just talking about to God, but to the man/woman of God as well? Saul was trying to literally execute David and David's words after having cut off just a piece of Saul's skirt was "...be it far from me to do this to the Lord's anointed." That right there servant is serving "As Unto the Lord."...when you are in a life-threatening situation because of your Man or Women of God and you can still conduct yourself wisely in all things. We never hear David say one negative thing about Saul during this whole ordeal. In other words, David never grumbled while he served. It is imperative that we take on the mindset of David...duck the javelin and take the kingdom, duck the javelin and take the kingdom are you hearing me duck the javelin and take the kingdom.

Lastly, the Bible says over in Hebrews 6:10 *"For God is not unrighteous to forget your work and labor of love, which ye have, showed toward his name, in that ye have ministered to the saints, and do minister."*

Listen child of God. Your services rendered will not be forgotten or go unrecognized. Even if you are not rewarded on this side, always remember that God has not forgotten about you, and God will bless you.

Chapter 3

Y'all Don't Hear Me
The Accounts of Miriam and Aaron

We are going to deal with three particular chapters, Numbers 12, 13, and 14. While all three have a common thread running through them, they are still somewhat different in context. Let's look at the first chapter in this trilogy found in Numbers 12:1-15...The accounts of Moses, Miriam, and Aaron.

Humble Yourself or God Will

Now this story is rather interesting, because it sounds like a scenario we deal within our churches today. There are those who tend to feel that they have the authority to speak whatever they feel necessary at the time, which is a great misconception on their part. It is obvious that Miriam and Aaron had a problem with the Ethiopian women whom Moses had married. If the truth were to be told, it sounds as if they may have been a bit on the racist side.

Listen servants, don't *ever* think that it is your place to *ever* tell the visionary what they should be doing or what you believe they are doing is wrong. Understand the question that Miriam and Aaron posed to Moses "Hath the Lord indeed spoken only by Moses? Hath he not spoken also by us? And the Lord heard it." I will admit that the Lord had not only spoken by Moses, I would be very wrong if I said that for there are scriptural accounts whereby God had spoken by others; however, God is not going to speak to you the same way He speaks to your Man or Women of God. Look what the Lord says in regards to that, "I will speak with him mouth to mouth, even clearly, and not in dark speeches." (Num. 12:8) There is a great distinction that God brings between the one who he has called to lead and to the one that is serving. We find that there is a great price to pay when one decides within themselves that are going to speak out against one of God's authority figures. The Bible says:

"Let every soul be subject to the higher authorities. For there is no authority but of God; the authorities that exist are ordained by God. So that the one resisting the authority resists the ordinance of God; and the ones who resist will receive judgment to themselves." Romans 13:1-2

As the story goes, God comes down and calls both Miriam and Aaron out to the front of the tent of meeting and rebukes them both. Once He departs we discover that Miriam became leprous. It is only after God's judgment is pronounced that Aaron then decides to beg for forgiveness. Now take a close look at the heart of a true pastor at work. Moses then immediately turns to God and begins to intercede on behalf of Miriam and the Lord says to Moses "If her father had but spit in her face, should she not be ashamed seven days? Let her be shut out from the camp seven days, and after that let her be received." (v.14) Now here it is that Moses was willing to forgive and forget; however, God says let her be ashamed and shut out the camp for seven days. And if we pay close attention to what transpired next, we find out that the camp did not move until she was received back after seven days. Listen closely; it is imperative that we be fully obedient and submitted to the governing authority in our lives. The entire camp is held up because of a young lady's elevated opinion of herself in the sight of God.

Your Ultimate Service Is To God

Let us look at this from another perspective. How many of us have gone to our respective workplaces and not fully obeyed the one in authority over us? Maybe we have had this thought somewhere in the inner recesses of our mind that because our boss is not saved we have felt that we did not have to submit to him or her. Allow me reiterate Romans 13:1 "Let every soul be submitting to higher [or, governing] authorities, for [there] is no authority except from God, but the existing authorities have been appointed by God." (ALT)

Now with that in mind, let me point out a few things that we can gather from this verse alone:
  1. ALL authority is from God
  2. ALL authority is appointed by God
  3. There is no indication of whether the authority should be saved or not.

The Bible says "Servants, be obedient unto them that according to the flesh are your masters, with fear and trembling, in singleness of your heart, as unto Christ; not in the way of eye-service, as men-pleasers; but as servants of Christ, doing the will of God from the heart..." (Ephesians. 6:5) The Bible tells us to reverently serve those who are our masters or those who rule over us with a sincere desire of wanting to do what is required, know that we are actually working for the Lord. Herein is the reason many of us get terminated from our jobs, it is simply because we work according to our flesh rather than according to the spirit of God that is in us.

Here is another harsh reality, our bosses do not care how well you can speak in tongues, quote scriptures, or cast out devils, they want to know that we are doing what the job requires at all times. Listen, I am not at all against those things; however, what does your job require? Now, if our bosses are paying us to do those things, then by all means we should do them to the best of our ability but if not, then let's keep things in their proper place.

The Bible further states:

"Servants, obey in all things your masters according to the flesh; not with eyeservice, as men pleasers; but in singleness of heart, fearing God: Whatsoever ye do, work heartily, as unto the Lord, and not unto men; knowing that from the Lord ye shall receive the recompense of the inheritance: ye serve the Lord Christ. For he that doeth wrong shall receive again for the wrong that he hath done: and there is no respect of persons." (Col. 3:22-25)

Now let us take a closer look at what this particular passage of scripture is saying to us:

1. Servants obey your master in all things—Servants must do the duty of the relation in which they stand, and obey their master's commands in all things which are consistent with their duty to God their heavenly Master.

2. Not just with eyeservice as men pleasers—not only when their master's eye is upon them, but also when they are from under their master's eye. They must be both just and diligent.

3. In singleness of heart, fearing God—without selfish designs, or hypocrisy and disguise.

4. And whatsoever you do, do it heartily—with diligence, not idly and slothfully:" or, "Do it cheerfully, not discontented.

5. As unto the Lord and not unto man—This sanctifies a servant's work when it is done as unto God.

6. Knowing that of the Lord you shall receive the reward of the inheritance, for you serve the Lord Christ—Serving your masters according to the command of Christ, you serve Christ, and he will be your paymaster:

Know Your Place

Lastly, I cannot stress enough the importance of our stance as it relates to serving in the ministry. We must keep our focus and make sure that the lines of authority don't ever get crossed. In other words, we need to make sure that we stay in our proper place until moved by the one(s) we serve. I will close with this passage of scripture found in Numbers 18:1-6.

Aaron, his sons, and his father's house have just been appointed by God to bear the iniquity of the priesthood. Also he is told to bring with him the tribe of Levi that they may minister unto him. God continues to give specific instruction stating that Levi shall keep their charge and the charge of the entire tabernacle. The thing that they should not do is come near the vessels of the sanctuary and the altar or else he (Levi) and Aaron would die. Pay close attention to the distinction God has just made between the one who is being served and the one that is serving. Levi's job is to take care of the sanctuary and make sure that it is ready for service and things of that nature.

He is never to come near the vessels of the sanctuary and the altar or else he and Aaron would die. Now, precautions should be taken so as not to get the duties mixed up. Levi, you do what Levi is supposed to do and Aaron, you do what Aaron is supposed to do. Levi does not ever need to make the mistake and think that he is in the priesthood or else he could be dead. That's what happens when people try to intrude on a calling that is not their own. They end up severely wounding or killing themselves as well as others. Take a look at the last thing God said in this passage. You who serve are given as gifts for the Lord... so the attitude should not be that they need you, no, you need to serve efficiently and effectively wherever you are planted until your time comes. And if by any chance you are not moved, Serve! Serve! Serve!

Chapter 4

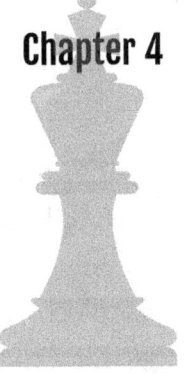

Glutton for Punishment
The Accounts of the Children of Israel

Here we will begin to deal with the second account of "Problem or Potential" as it relates to Moses and the Children of Israel. When we consider leading ourselves...while there is the chance for things to possibly go wrong, we don't necessarily have to deal with the negative kickback we would get when we're leading a group of people such as the Children of Israel.

As we saw in Numbers 12 the total disrespect to authority, this particular passage in Chapter 14 of Numbers is very interesting as well. We see the continuing complaining of the children of Israel. It would seem to me that after all that God did for them in regards to sending them a deliver, performing all those miracles while they were still slaves, providing manna for them to eat, guiding them by a cloud by day and a pillar of fire by night, parting the Red Sea and after they saw what happened to Miriam, you would think that would have been enough to prove that He (God) is able to take care of and sustain them and that He is not one to play with. Unfortunately, like the children of Israel some people just have to learn the hard way.

Have You Lost Your Mind?

What in the world was going on in the minds of the Children of Israel? Here it is that they have come through various hurdles and yet still want to complain about their situation. They make the statement "Would to God that we had died in the land of Egypt! or "Would to God that we had died in this wilderness!" (v.2) More importantly than that, they decide among themselves to appoint another leader to escort them back into bondage. "And they said one to another, Let us make a captain, and let us return into Egypt." (v.4) Now they murmured, cried and complained while they were in bondage. God sends them a deliverer by way of Moses who is leading them to their freedom and now because it is not going the way they want it to, they want to return to the land of their affliction. Let me add this one little footnote, God can successfully bring us out of something that we were in bondage to; however, if we are not free from that thing in the inner recesses of our mind then we will ultimately go back to that very thing. Consider this quote:

"If you can control a man's thinking you do not have to worry about his action. When you determine what a man shall think you do not have to concern yourself about what he will do. If you make a man feel that he is inferior, you do not have to compel him to accept an inferior status, for he will seek it himself. If you make a man think that he is justly an outcast, you do not have to order him to the back door. He will go without being told; and if there is no back door, his very nature will demand one." ~Cater G. Woodson

How do you give up something that you are used to being

in? Yes, the children of Israel complained about being in bondage, but they were used to being in it. You may ask the question "why would you say that Bro. Jesse?" Look at the statement they made "Let us make a captain, and let us return into Egypt." here is the word for which they were INSTITUTIONALIZED meaning "lacking the will or ability to think and act independently because of having spent a long time in an institution such as a psychiatric hospital or prison." They had grown accustomed to being bondage so much so that it infiltrated their minds.

<u>Don't Follow the Crowd</u>

It is after that the children of Israel make that statement that Moses and Aaron fall on their faces before the assembly and that Joshua and Caleb rip their clothes and begin to speak to the children of Israel. They simply state that the land that they passed through was good and if the Lord delighted in them then He would give it to them. Pay close attention to the next statement that Joshua and Caleb say to the Children of Israel. "Only rebel not ye against the LORD…" Wait a minute, they were complaining against Moses and Aaron, but Joshua and Caleb say "Rebel not against the Lord" It is interesting to note that even after that, the children of Israel still are in an uproar so much so that now they want to stone Joshua and Caleb. It is then that the Glory of the Lord appears and begins to speak with Moses.

Here is the question God ask Moses when the glory of the Lord appears, "How long will this people provoke me? and how long will it be ere they believe me, for all the signs which I have showed among them?" (v.11). Now that question becomes very significant because the accounts of the children of Israel clearly point to them complaining against Moses and Aaron, but God sees it differently. Do you remember the passage of scripture in

Romans 13:1-2 about all authority coming from God?

"LET EVERY person be loyally subject to the governing (civil) authorities. For there is no authority except from God [by His permission, His sanction], and those that exist do so by God's appointment. Therefore he who resists and sets himself up against the authorities resists what God has appointed and arranged [in divine order]. And those who resist will bring down judgment upon themselves [receiving the penalty due them]." (Roman 13:1-2 Amp)

<u>The Revealing of the Pastor's Heart</u>

It is after God posed the question to Moses that He says "I will smite them with the pestilence, and disinherit them, and will make of thee a greater nation and mightier than they." (v.12). Pastors tell me if that doesn't sound good right there. God said he would get rid of the whole congregation and give Moses a greater nation and mightier one than the one that is presently with him. Now how many pastors have not thought about that very thing right there? God give me some people that I can work with and count on. However, despite God's offer Moses begins to intercede for the people. It is in Moses' conversation with God, that we see the true heart of a pastor at work in versus 13-19 in Numbers 14.

The only reason that the children of Israel were able to remain alive was due to the true pastor's heart of Moses. Listen, those of us who serve and work in our various ministries, we need to learn to be mindful of what we say and keep our mouth off of the Men and Women of God for it is their prayers for us that help sustain us the midst of our stubborn, rebellious, selfish mindsets and attitudes. Even in the midst of these people complaining acting a fool, Moses still wanted the best for them and was constantly willing to stand in the gap on their behalf.

Hear the case that Moses presented to God as it relates to the children of Israel, Moses says God, if you kill these people off then not only will the Egyptians hear about it but ALL the inhabitants of the land will hear about it too. He says the inhabitants already know that you are among the Children of Israel and if they hear that you were able to bring them out of the land of their affliction, but not able to bring them into the land in which you swore unto them, so you killed them in the wilderness what will they say of you then? He goes on to say, let the power of the Lord be great who is LONG SUFFERING and of GREAT MERCY. Now just pause right there and let's deal with these two words, LONG SUFFERING and GREAT MERCY.

I personally thank God that he is LONG SUFFERING and has GREAT MERCY, for the things that I have done. I should have been cut off a long time ago. I don't want you to read this book and think that I am free from being guilty of not doing anything wrong...No. I was messed up and it's amazing that God could work with such a mess. Listen HE is LONG SUFFERING and HIS MERCY is GREAT. Long Suffering means to "SUFFER LONG". The connotation in which it is used here means slow to anger. GREAT MERCY simply implies not getting what we really deserve. SO in essence we could say "Let the power of the Lord be great...who is slow to anger and not giving us what we really deserve". Listen, he goes on to say "forgiving iniquity and transgression, and by no means clearing the guilty..." Here is the part that I love most, Moses asks the Lord to pardon the people and it is plainly obvious to see that the only reason why the Lord withheld his hand was and I quote "the LORD said, I have pardoned according to thy word." Look at the heart of a pastor at work in this Man of God. How many times have we at some time or another risen up against the authority of the house and the only reason why God withheld his judgment was because the Man or Woman of God stepped in and said God "YOU KNOW".

Chapter 5

Friend or Foe
The Accounts of Korah

In this final look of, "Problem or Potential," we will consider the accounts of Moses and Korah. As God's servants, it is necessary to pay close attention to this section.

The book of Numbers Chapter 16:1-50 gives us a detailed account regarding the heart and mind of one of God's servants. As we delve into this story you will discover a few things present in the servant Korah.

This passage becomes interesting because you would think that by now that the Children of Israel would have gotten the point that it is not a good idea to come against the Man of God. Unfortunately, just like the children of Israel, despite how much God shows us the consequences of rebelling against his authority, we still do so because of our selfish pride. If you were to look at this passage of scripture just at face value, one could assume that all Korah was trying to do was to alleviate some of the pressure off of Moses. However, if we take a closer look at the motive behind what Korah was saying, we begin to see a very different picture. Allow me to point out that this was the cousin of Moses. I stated in an earlier chapter, it is not always the people outside of the church (family) who cause problems. Moses' problems primarily came from his family. Have you ever had that individual be it family or not try to disguise themselves as one who really cares, but when it was all said and done, they were only out for themselves? Such is the case for Moses in this final part of the trilogy "Problem or Potential."

Ulterior Motives

Korah, after they gather an assembly against Moses and Aaron makes the statement:

"Ye take too much upon you, seeing all the congregation are holy, every one of them, and the LORD is among them: wherefore then lift ye up yourselves above the congregation of the LORD?"

Now I will go as far as to say that the statement that Korah made was true. Moses did have a lot on his plate; however, I am concerned with the motive in which the statement was made. Korah was not at all concerned with the fact that Moses had a lot going on, he was however concerned with gaining position and notoriety. Here in is one of the problems I have with Korah. Where was he when all the Children of Israel were crying out for a deliver? Where was he when the Egyptian was beating one of the Israelites? Where was he when Moses and Aaron stood before Pharaoh? It almost appears that now that all the major issues have passed that he now wants to step up and be in charge.

I believe the word that best describes Korah's statement is "Motive." Motive is defined as:

Something that causes a person to act in a certain way, do a certain thing, etc.; incentive. The goal or object of a person's actions.

So as we begin to look at Korah, I want us to do a self-examination on ourselves as well to see whether or not we are serving for the right reasons. As I said earlier, I am sure that Moses did have a lot on his plate...show me a pastor who does not, particularly one who is a visionary. Moses had people murmuring and complaining, building idol gods, and constantly challenging his authority just to name a few. It was so bad that even God himself wanted to wipe the people out and some he did! Allow me, if you will, to ask just a few questions. What's the primary reason we want or desire the position? Is it to get notoriety? Is it to prove that we think we can do a better job than our pastor can? Is it to show up someone we are in competition with? Were we there when the times got rough? All these question and more are very essential when it comes to serving. There must be a clear examination into the heart and mind of the individual to see if they are lining up with one another. The scripture says: "... For out of the fullness (the overflow, the super abundance) of the heart the mouth speaks." (Matthew.12:34^b Amp.) I want us to understand that before it is all said and done...the true motives of a person's nature will be revealed, just as in the case with Korah. As I said earlier, Korah's statement may have been right; however, it was the motive behind his statement that made it wrong.

Dividing Asunder

I want us to take a look at one last passage of scripture as we conclude. I believe this will help to summarize all that I am conveying to you. Hebrews 4:12-13 (AMP)

"For the Word that God speaks is alive and full of power [making it active, operative, energizing, and effective]; it is sharper than any two-edged sword, penetrating to the dividing line of the breath of life (soul) and [the immortal] spirit, and of joints and marrow [of the deepest parts of our nature], exposing and sifting and analyzing and judging the very

thoughts and purposes of the heart. And not a creature exists that is concealed from His sight, but all things are open and exposed, naked and defenseless to the eyes of Him with Whom we have to do."

We must examine our motives when it comes to serving God as well as the men and women of God. This scripture clearly indicates that there is nothing hid from God. The Word is able to pierce through every part of our natural being. I want us to hone in on the section that addresses that the Word of God is so powerful that it exposes, sifts, analyzes and judges the very thoughts and purposes of the heart. In other words, our motive will be exposed whether good or bad. And the later part of that scripture says EVERYONE and EVERYTHING is laid open naked to him we have to give an account to.

Child of God, apostle, prophet, evangelist, pastor, teacher... servant. We need to make sure that we do not fall into the situations that Aaron, Miriam, The Children of Israel and Korah fell into. Understand who you are serving and why you serving, thus helping to keep your motives pure before God.

Chapter 6

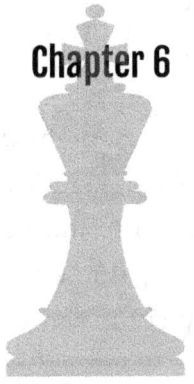

Integrity Issues

> *"And Achan answered Joshua, and said, indeed I have sinned against the Lord, the God of Israel, and thus and thus have I done: When I saw among the spoils a goodly Babylonish garment, and two hundred shekels of silver and a wedge of gold of fifty shekels weight, then I coveted them, and took them; behold, they are hid in the earth in the midst of my tent, and the silver underneath it."*
> Joshua 7: 20-21 KJV

Integrity defined by Merriam-Webster is "the quality of being honest and having strong moral principles; moral uprightness." According to his book "American Religion Contemporary Trends" Professor Mark Chaves of Duke University a professor of sociology, religion and divinity, found that between 1973 and 2008, the percentage of people with "great confidence" in religious leaders declined from 35 percent to less than 25 percent.

It is sad to think that in today's society, if you surveyed many people, you will discover that many have lost confidence in the church. Now I want to clarify that when I say the church...I'm referring to the people, not the building. I really don't want to go into all the many excuses as to why people don't go; however, if you pay close attention to what is being said, it all boils down to the issue of Integrity.

Now because I want to be just in my dealings, I could rightfully say that there is an integrity issue with those who have made the decision to point fingers absent accepting any responsibility for themselves as to why they don't attend. With all that being said, let's deal with the issue of integrity inside Joshua's camp as well as our various places of worship.

I am sure all of us, at some point and time, have read about Joshua or at least heard about him. Joshua was Moses front man; he was the one that Moses turned to in the time of need. If Moses needed something done, he'd send Joshua because Joshua was a man of action. Joshua was the type of individual that wasn't going to do a whole lot of talking, particularly in battle. If you remember, Joshua was the one in Joshua Chapter 5:13 who ran up on the angel with his sword drawn asking "Art thou for us, or for our adversaries?" You know he has either got to be a bad or just plain crazy to run up on an angel of the Lord at that the captain of the host of the Lord. This is the type of person Joshua was; he was of good moral character and of utmost loyal integrity.

Sin Within the Camp

So here we have it in chapter 7 of the book of Joshua, based on the report given to him by his men after scouting Ai, he only sends a hand full of men to do battle with Ai. Ai from his scouting party's report is not that worthy of an adversary whereby Joshua should send his entire army, so they say send only about two or three thousand. Upon the advice of his scouts, Joshua does so and his army is utterly defeated. In the process of trying to escape, the men of Ai killed about 36 of Joshua's men while the rest flee for their lives.

Have you ever been in a battle, going into one or maybe not a battle but a situation whereby you knew beyond a shadow of a doubt that the odds were completely in your favor, yet when the dust settled and the smoke cleared you stood on the losing end, humiliated and morally defeated? Such is the case here with Joshua. This was supposed to be an assured victory but as we can see, he was utterly defeated and no doubt as the scriptures tells us, just a tad bit perplexed as to why he lost what should have been an easy victory. Hear what Joshua's response is to the battle lost:

"And Joshua rent his clothes, and fell to the earth upon his face before the ark of the LORD until the eventide, he and the elders of Israel, and put dust upon their heads. And Joshua said, Alas, O Lord GOD, wherefore hast thou at all brought this people over Jordan, to deliver us into the hand of the Amorites, to destroy us? would to God we had been content, and dwelt on the other side Jordan! O Lord, what shall I say, when Israel turneth their backs before their enemies! For the Canaanites and all the inhabitants of the land shall hear of it, and shall environ us round, and cut off our name from the earth: and what wilt thou do unto thy great name?" Joshua 7:6-9

We are hearing the sincere hearts cry of Joshua after he lost the battle and his concern is what the enemy of the Lord's people will do. Yet, while the concern maybe heartfelt from Joshua's point of view, the Lord sees it very differently. Have you ever been in a place of sincere prayer, pouring out your heart to God expecting to be comforted by some reassuring words and the Lord just flips the script on you? Well that is exactly the case here with Joshua. This is how God responded to Joshua's prayer:

"And the LORD said unto Joshua, Get thee up; wherefore liest thou thus upon thy face? Israel hath sinned, and they have also transgressed

my covenant which I commanded them: for they have even taken of the accursed thing, and have also stolen, and disassembled also, and they have put it even among their own stuff. Therefore, the children of Israel could not stand before their enemies, but turned their backs before their enemies, because they were accursed: neither will I be with you any more, except ye destroy the accursed from among you. Up, sanctify the people, and say, Sanctify yourselves against to morrow: for thus saith the LORD God of Israel, There is an accursed thing in the midst of thee, O Israel: thou canst not stand before thine enemies, until ye take away the accursed thing from among you." Joshua 7:10-13

I'm not going to say that God completely ignores the prayer of Joshua; however, he says we have something more serious to deal with than just what you're inquiring about. God tells him that Israel has sinned by taking of the "accursed" thing which is the reason why you cannot stand in victory before your enemies. This thing must be dealt with immediately or I the Lord will cease to be with you except you destroy the "accursed" thing. While there are many things we do not want the Lord to say to us…I am sure that ranks as one of the top ten statements you never want to hear the Lord say "I will cease to be with you." There are many instances when the Lord has declared that he will cease to be with someone. The story of King Saul found in 1 Samuel 15:1-29 is a great example.

Are You There Lord?

The Lord ceased to be with King Saul after he have disobeyed the commandment of the Lord. King Saul feared (was scared of) the people more than he feared (reverenced) God, thus causing him to do things that would please man rather than please God, and it ultimately cost him the kingdom as well as his life. It is important to obey the voice of the Lord in all that we do. While

Joshua did not directly disobey the voice of the Lord, one of his men did, which lead to their humiliating defeat against Ai. If we look closely at the story we see that not only was Achan held accountable for his actions, but Joshua was also held accountable for the actions of his tribe members.

This gives very good reference to the book of Revelations in which the Lord deals with the Angel (Pastor) of the churches. You will discover in the book of Revelations that there are issues going on in six of the seven churches. The Lord compliments the works that they are doing, yet there are some things that he has against them. While not all the issues surrounding the churches are not necessarily the fault of the Angel (pastor) of the church, he addresses them because they are the ones set over the church. This is the situation facing Joshua, one of his members has sinned, taken of the "accursed" thing and hid it amongst his possessions. In doing so, it cost Israel a battle and the lives of some of their men.

The Lord gives Joshua very specific instructions on what to do the next morning. He brings Israel up by tribes until Achan is standing before him according to Joshua 7:19-23.

There's a Thief Among Us

Now I would like to take the time out to applaud Achan for being honest with Joshua and for not trying to hide it from him; however, integrity would have said that the best thing would have been not to have taken of the "accursed" things in the first place. It is sad to think that this man's selfish, greedy attitude and lack of integrity would eventually not only cost him his life but also the life of his entire family as we see in Joshua 7:24-26.

"And Joshua, and all Israel with him, took Achan the son of Zerah, and the silver, and the garment, and the wedge of gold, and his sons, and

his daughters, and his oxen, and his asses, and his sheep, and his tent, and all that he had: and they brought them unto the valley of Achor. And Joshua said, Why hast thou troubled us? The LORD shall trouble thee this day. And all Israel stoned him with stones, and burned them with fire, after they had stoned them with stones. And they raised over him a great heap of stones unto this day. So the LORD turned from the fierceness of his anger. Wherefore the name of that place was called, The valley of Achor, unto this day." Joshua 7:24-26

As we can see here, Joshua and the entire tribe of Israel not only stone Achan, but his entire family. And as we can see the Lord wanted nothing of Achan to remain. They destroyed everything that was connected to Achan in any way: wife, children, oxen, asses, sheep, tent...everything. I wonder what the world would be like today if we operated on the same principles as Joshua did. How many of us would be here today? Would you be reading this book...would this book have ever been written? Bless God for the saving grace of our Lord and Savior Jesus the Christ.

The issue of integrity within the body of Christ, particularly when it comes to serving in the house of God is so vastly important that the life of the ministry hangs on its hinges. As we see in Joshua's encampment and in Saul's life, the issue of integrity was key and ultimately played a significant part in their demise.

Chapter 7

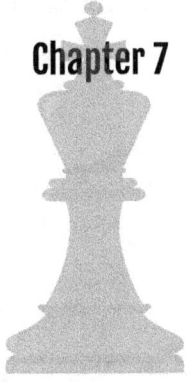

A Cancerous Cell

You were perfect in your ways from the day that you were created, until iniquity was found in you.
(Ezekiel 28.15)

For you have said in your heart, I will go up to the heavens, I will exalt my throne above the stars of God; I will also sit on the mount of the congregation, in the sides of the north.
I will go up above the heights of the clouds;
I will be like the Most High.
(Isaiah 14:13-14)

The Cancer Within

Cancer as defined by the Mayo Clinic: "refers to any one of a large number of diseases characterized by the development of abnormal cells that divide uncontrollably and have the ability to infiltrate and destroy normal body tissue." In simple terms, cancer occurs when abnormal cells in a part(s) of the body begin to grow out of control. One abnormal cell becomes two, two become four, and four become eight, and so on, until a mass of cells (a tumor) is created. The tumor interferes with the normal functioning of healthy tissue and can spread to other parts of your body. Cancer invades and destroys normal tissue and it can also produce chemicals that interfere with body functions.

Normal cells divide and grow in an orderly fashion, but cancer cells do not. They continue to grow and crowd out normal cells. Most cells in the human body have a certain lifespan and they stop multiplying or eventually die off, which is the reason our body keeps producing cells; however, this is not the case with cancer cells. They are "abnormal cells gone wild." They do not have built within them the mechanism that says stop multiplying, so they just keep growing and reproducing after their own kind until they take over or at least try. I would classify Satan as an "abnormal cell" that rebelled, was out of control, infiltrated a third of the angels, and still reproduces after his kind today. So, as we continue to address the subject of servanthood, I want us to take into consideration what are some "cancerous cells" to the body:

Pride
Jealousy
Envy
Hatred
Bitterness
Malice
Strife

A Perfectly Imperfect Creation

I want us to read Ezekiel 28:13-19 and Isaiah 14:12-19 as we continue to address to subject of servanthood.

It is very important we examine ourselves when it comes to serving in a capacity of leadership. We must make sure that we do not allow ourselves to become or get infected by a cancerous cell. In the scriptures mentioned at the beginning, we discover what caused Satan to be kicked out of heaven. Pride, envy and vain glory can be an awful thing to have take hold of us. It is obvious that these were the characteristic that defined Satan himself. However, let's look a little closer at what God says about him:

"...*every precious stone was your covering, the ruby, topaz, and the diamond, the beryl, the onyx, and the jasper, the sapphire, the turquoise, and the emerald, and gold. The workmanship of your tambourines and of your flutes was prepared in you in the day that you were created ... You were perfect in your ways from the day that you were created, until iniquity was found in you.*"(28:13&15)

Listen, God said that there was not a blemish in him until iniquity was found there. Let me ask you a question, WHAT'S GROWING in you? Apparently there had to be something growing in Satan otherwise, he would have not sinned against God. Look at what the Bible says about the growth of sin and what it leads to.

"*But every man is tempted, when he is drawn away of his own lust, and enticed. Then when lust hath conceived, it bringeth forth sin: and sin, when it is finished, bringeth forth death.*"(James 1:15-15)

Did you notice the growing process that occurs? First there is the temptation (a craving or desire for something, especially something thought wrong) then the drawing away by his own lust (the strong physical desire to have sex with somebody, usually without associated feelings of love or affection, intense sexual desire or appetite; uncontrolled or illicit sexual desire or appetite; lecherousness. A passionate or overmastering desire or craving) and after having been and drawn by lust, he is enticed (lured, inveigled or allured). It goes on to say that when this unnatural and unhealthy desire has conceived (produce something in the mind whereby action has been put to it), it brings forth sin and when the sin is full grown or has reached maturity it brings forth death.

Now if we just use our "sanctified imagination" for just a moment, I could imagine him being the most decorated of all angels. Everywhere he went all the other angels would look in awe at him because of his beauty. When he would open his mouth to sing My God!! The melodious sounds that would stream from his innermost being would just probably be breathtaking . Not to mention that he was *"The"* anointed cherub that covers and was placed on the holy height of God and walked up and down in the midst of the stones of fire. He had it all, the anointing, beauty, fame, what else could he ask for? Oh that's right he wanted to be GOD. So he starts promoting himself instead of God or should I say his pastor. Ezekiel 28:16 says

"By the multitude of thy merchandise they have filled the midst of thee with violence, and thou hast sinned..."

You know "I" have noticed that pastor doesn't handle things the way he/she used to. You know if "I" were the pastor "I" wouldn't do things like that. "I" believe that pastor is behind in the times and some changes need to be made. "I" believe that he/she is trying to do too much and should sit down. Do some of those things sound familiar? Here is a better question, have we said some of those things ourselves? Have there been times we have tried to exalt our "throne" above that of our Man or Women of God? Have there been times we have spread our filthy, vicious lies just to steal the hearts of others from our pastor?

Puff, Puff...Tumble, Tumble

You know there is a very interesting passage of scripture in 2 Samuel 15:1-6 that deals with David's son Absalom.

"And it came to pass after this, that Absalom prepared him chariots and horses, and fifty men to run before him. And Absalom rose up early, and stood beside the way of the gate: and it was so, that when any man that had a controversy came to the king for judgment, then Absalom called unto him, and said, Of what city art thou? And he said, Thy servant is of one of the tribes of Israel. And Absalom said unto him, See, thy matters are good and right; but there is no man deputed of the king to hear thee. Absalom said moreover, Oh that I were made judge in the land, that every man which hath any suit or cause might come unto me, and I would do him justice! And it was so, that when any man came nigh to him to do him obeisance, he put forth his hand, and took him, and kissed him. And on this manner did Absalom to all Israel that came to the king for judgment: so Absalom stole the hearts of the men of Israel."

I once heard a pastor from Oklahoma say "Puff, Puff, Tumble, Tumble," which is a paraphrase of the scripture *"Pride comes before destruction and a haughty spirit before a fall"* (Proverbs 16:18)

The Apostle Peter tells us: "Likewise, you who are younger and of lesser rank, be subject to the elders (the ministers and spiritual guides of the church) - [giving them due respect and yielding to their counsel]. Clothe (apron) yourselves, all of you, with humility [as the garb of a servant, so that is covering cannot possibly be stripped from you, with freedom from pride and arrogance] toward one another. For God sets Himself against the proud (the insolent, the overbearing, the disdainful, the presumptuous, the boastful)—[and He opposes, frustrates, and defeats them], but gives grace favor blessing) to the humble." (1 Peter 5:5 AMP.)

As I stated earlier pride, envy and vainglory can be an awful thing to let get hold of you. In the case of Satan, it cost him getting kicked out of heaven and in the case of Absalom; it eventually cost him his life. Pride causes one to lose status and position as we see in the case of Satan in Isaiah 14:19

"But thou art cast out of thy grave like an abominable branch, and as the raiment of those that are slain, thrust through with a sword, that go down to the stones of the pit; as a carcase trodden under feet."

It is obvious that in these scenarios, both Satan and Absalom were blinded by their own pride. My Bishop always says that if you tell a lie long enough, you will eventually start to believe it yourself. It is very sad to think that we can become so blinded by the lies we tell ourselves. In its simplest form, a lie is a false misconception about one's self. Pride also weakens the overall body of Christ. The Bible says that Satan weakened the nations. We that are servants, pastors, leaders etc. cannot afford to operate in the spirit of pride for very serious consequences will follow.

Build Your Spiritual Immune System

Cancerous cells are sometimes very difficult to get rid of depending on the severity of the situation and what stage the individual is in. It not only places that particular part of the body in jeopardy, but the body as a whole. We find that Satan infected one-third of the angels in heaven thus getting them put out of heaven just as he was. Let's consider what the Apostle Paul tells us about each part of the body of Christ (the church) contributing for the overall success:

"Under his control all the different parts of the body fit together, and the whole body is held together by every joint with which it is provided. So when each separate part works as it should the whole body grows and builds itself up through love." (Ephesians 4:16 GNB)

We should not even begin to think that the local church body, not to mention the overall body of Christ is going to be effective with cancerous cells running rampant in it's midst. Look very close to what the preceding scripture said, " ... So when each separate part WORKS AS IT SHOULD the WHOLE BODY GROWS and BUILDS ITSELF UP ... "

The time has come for us to stop playing around and being so lackadaisical in our serving. In much simpler terms the time has come for us to grow up. It is not about us or what we think should be done or not. God did not send us to our particular pastor because he/she needed our help. Believe me; God, our pastor and the vision will not cease to exist if we are not there.

For those of us who serve, we must understand that the only way for the ministry to grow is not to build the ministry first but to build the people and in turn the people will build the ministry. Yes, the ministry of help, especially the area of servanthood is very important, but in order for us to operate at the level in which God intends, there must be a level of understanding on both the pastor as well as the servant.

Chapter 8

Captivated Heart

And Elisha cried ... My father, My father ...
(2 Kings 2:12)

Have you ever wondered what goes on in the heart of an individual who has committed his or her life to serve their pastor(s), and then one day instead of considering them their "master", they call them father? The story of Elijah and Elisha is one that is very close to my heart for personal reasons, to which I will refer as I go throughout this chapter. However, I do believe it to be necessary for us to look back at how this relationship came into being in order for us to get a clear understanding of the Captivated Heart of Elisha.

Captivated Heart

One of the foremost national and international leadership development speakers of this age is Dr. Les Brown. I had the pleasure of sitting in his presence and gleaning nuggets from his teachings on numerous occasions. During one of his sessions on "Overcoming Fear" he stated:

> *"Wanting something is not enough. You must hunger for it. Your motivation must be absolutely compelling in order to overcome the obstacles that will invariably come your way."*
>
> ~Les Brown~

As we delve into the life of Elisha, we will see his hunger and motivation be put to the test as he commits to walk out with what he believes is his divine calling from God.

In 1 Kings 19: 19 we discover that Elisha is plowing in the field when Elijah passes by and throws his mantle upon him. Elisha then immediately runs after Elijah and says

"Let me, I pray thee, kiss my father and mother, and then will follow thee."

Elijah's response is *"Go back again: what have I done to thee?"* This seems to be somewhat of a hard statement. What we must realize here is that Elijah could have told Elisha what to do, however, that would have possibly been Elisha doing something because he was told to and not because he wanted to. We need to make sure that we are not simply operating off the mere fact that we are being told what to do. If that were the case, then I would venture to say that we would have some men and women who are only modeling the standard of a modernized slave. The decision to follow Elijah had to be 100% Elisha's and no one else.

Now allow me to clear an erroneous belief as it relates to Elisha's response to Elijah. There some who believe that because Elisha asked to go back and kiss his father and mother that this is indicative of one who after having heard the word turns and falls away. Allow me to say that this is not even close to being the truth at all. Let us look closely at the course of action Elisha took as he prepared to follow Elijah. While Elisha did ask to go back and kiss his father and mother, the Bible does not give any indication that he did such a thing.

"And he returned back from him, and took the yoke of oxen, and slew them, and boiled their flesh with the instruments the oxen, and gave unto the people, and they did eat. Then he arose, and went after Elijah, and ministered unto him." (1 Kings 19:21 KJV)

The scripture is very clear in that Elisha gave up what he had in order to follow the man of God. Why does the scripture not tell us whether he kisses his father and mother? While there may be a lot of reason as to why, allow me to put this one out there. Understand that Elisha was not a poor man neither did he come from a poor family. Furthermore, if we understand Elijah's history, we discover that he was a wanderer or vagabond if you will. He had no stability in regards to where he stayed nor does it appear that he had a lot of money and yet Elisha chooses to give up everything to follow what seems to be an unstable man. Now here is a question for you. How many parents do you think would agree to that type of decision? Therefore, I submit to you that I do not necessarily believe that Elisha's parents were in total agreement with his decision to follow Elijah. Despite what it cost him, Elisha chose to go and minister to Elijah.

Now, if we pay close attention to the next few chapters of 1 Kings 20:1-2, we discover that Elisha is nowhere to be found. It is almost as if Elisha goes into seclusion, something like Christ did when he disappeared for 18 years although it was not that long for Elisha. There is discussion about Elijah and another prophet, but there is no indication that, that prophet is Elisha. Elisha pops back on the scene in 2 Kings 2: 1, Elijah is going to be taken up by a whirlwind into heaven, but before this takes place Elijah is sent to three different places: Bethel, Jericho, and Jordan. We first see that Elijah tries to tell Elisha to remain behind while he goes on, but Elisha's response becomes very important as it relates to what lies ahead. Elisha says *"As the LORD liveth, and thy soul liveth,! I will not leave thee."* Secondly, we discover that there were prophets at all three of these places and all of them had the same mindset when it came to Elijah and Elisha; not one of those prophets considered Elijah to be their master. It is understood that Elijah is the "top" prophet at that time; however, none of the prophets at Bethel, Jericho or Jordan considered Elijah to be their master. The emphasis on the question that they posed to Elisha was *"Do you know that the Lord will take away your master (speaking of Elijah) from you today?"* Allow me to say this for the benefit of those that are committed to serving their man or woman of God. It is not always the people outside of the ministry that will try to distract or challenge you in regards to what God has called you to do. Notice that these were prophets that were speaking to Elisha and they were not speaking falsely; their statements were very true, Elijah was going to be taken away from him. However, what is key here is the way Elisha chooses to respond to what is being said to him. Elisha says *"Yea, I know; hold ye your peace."* In other words, he says I already know what is going to happen, Shut Up about it. Now listen closely, there will be times when the word of prophecy will come to you, how you choose to respond will determine the after affects that you will have to deal with.

The Jordan River Walk Experience

As Elijah and Elisha come to the Jordan, Elijah takes off his Mantle and strikes the water, the waters divide, and they walk across on dry land. I am not very concerned with the length and width of the Jordan River; we just need to know that it took some time for them to get across. The Bible does not give any indication of what took place while they were crossing this river. I would like to point out that while Elisha was on the other side of the Jordan and the prophets were saying "Don't you know the Lord will take your master way from you?" Elisha said, "Yes, I know keep silent." Something very interesting had to happen while they were crossing the Jordan. I am sure that both Elijah and Elisha had a chance to share their hearts with one another and in doing so, something happened in the heart of Elisha that change his perspective of how he saw Elijah.

Now pay close attention to what has and is about to transpire after they have crossed the Jordan. Elijah asked "What is it that I can do for you, before I am taken away?" Elisha response is that he (Elijah) let a double portion of his spirit be upon him (Elisha). In essence, he is asking for the same right and/or privileges of a firstborn son. Elijah's response to him is that he has asked a hard thing; nevertheless, if Elisha sees him when he is taken then it will be so, but if not then it will not be.

Looking intently so as not to miss anything as they walked on, Elisha cries... *"My father, my father..."* Notice the difference in how Elisha sees Elijah after they cross the Jordan. Before they come to the Jordan, the prophets at the various places asked him *"Do you not know your Master will be taken from you?"* Elisha never corrects them and says he is not my master. Yet while there is no correction on the part of Elisha, sometimes it's not even worth your time trying to correct someone that is bent on operating in their ignorance. Elisha was after something and had no time to deal with gossipy onlookers. While crossing the Jordan, I believe something transpired in the heart of Elisha that captivated his heart whereby he no longer saw a master but a father.

I stated earlier chapter that I would go into more depth in regards to why this particular passage of scripture is so dear to me. While in college, at Grambling State University, I came across an individual who greatly affected and effected my life in a tremendous way. So as not to drag my experience out, I will share a condensed version of how my life was changed. My years at Grambling State University were long, needless to say very long, but I would not change anything. Upon coming close to the end of my first year there, I met my man by the name of Bennett Smith who at the time was the campus minister; little did I know that he would eventually become my "Elijah" who became my father. As the years went on we developed a relationship that was questioned by many, but like Elisha, I knew in my spirit something greater was coming out of it. So, despite what the critics and the distant onlookers were saying I was determined to keep my focus. He eventually left Grambling while I was still there and went back to his hometown.

During this time, another pastor would try to step in; however, he was not my Elijah. There came a time when Bennett and I were talking that he informed me of a conversation that he had with this pastor. The outcome was not good, but in the midst of that, his statement to me would change my perspective of him from that day on. His words, as simple as they were, had a profound effect on me. He stated, "You do whatever you have to do and obey God. If that means cutting me off and cutting him off, you obey God." From that moment, I knew that he was not out for personal gain and that my well-being was a priority to him. It was at that moment that Elijah was no longer my "master" but became my Father.

As I end this chapter, I want to share with you some real life stories from others that had a "Jordan River Walk Experience" with their Elijah/Father. These stories will be located in the back of this book for your reading.

Chapter 9

The Role of Spiritual Fathers

"I write not these things to shame you, but as my beloved sons I warn you. For though ye have ten thousand instructors in Christ, yet have ye not many fathers: for in Christ Jesus I have begotten you through the gospel. Wherefore I beseech you, be ye followers of me. For this cause have I sent unto you Timothy, who is my beloved son, and faithful in the Lord, who shall bring you into remembrance of my ways which be in Christ, as I teach everywhere in every church. Now some are puffed up, as though I would not come to you. But I will come to you shortly, if the Lord will, and will know, not the speech of them which are puffed up, but the power. For the kingdom of God is not in word, but in power. What will ye? shall I come unto you with a rod, or in love, and in the spirit of meekness?" (1 Corinthians 4:14-21 KJV)

One of the sad hallmarks of our individualistic society today is a growing irresponsibility. While we see this issue permeating within several areas socially, it is tragically obvious in the area of parenting. It manifests itself in parents who fail to take responsibility for raising their children and in men who father children and then walk away from them. What is operating within us that makes us selfish and irresponsible? Has sin so infected our sensibilities that we can let innocent children suffer want so that we ourselves can be more comfortable and satisfied? Clearly, the answer is yes, it has.

It is no wonder, then, that when we come to Christ; we must unlearn a number of behavior patterns, and replace them with a proper understanding of how to live in selfless and responsible ways. This rings especially true in the area of relationships.

In our text, we discover that Paul gives insight into what characterizes a spiritual father, or one who takes responsibility for young Christian's spiritual growth. We see that there are several markings of a spiritual father:

- Spiritual Fathers Warn in Love
- Spiritual Fathers Reproduces Life
- Spiritual Fathers Set an Example
- Spiritual Fathers Teach
- Spiritual Fathers Discipline

These character traits should inspire us, both men and women, to rise to the challenge of becoming one who can nurture others in their walk with God. I want us to look more closely at these traits as it relates to our fathers or those of us on the verge of becoming fathers.

A Spiritual Father Warns in Love

"I write not these things to shame you, but as my beloved sons I warn you." (1 Corinthians 4:14 KJV)

Perhaps the greatest characteristic of parents is their love for their children. A parent without love is defective. If you were describing a machine, you would say, "It's broken. It doesn't work right!" Parents who do not love don't work right inside. They need to be fixed. Normal parents love their children. It is out of that love for our children that we take responsibility for them, for their care and feeding, for their welfare and safety, for their training and maturity. It is because of love that we care whether they do what is right and avoid what is wrong or hurtful. One of the characteristics of being a spiritual father is that a spiritual father warns his children in love. Paul calls them his dear children. Like any good parent, as soon as he saw them he loved them. They were dear to him. He cared about their welfare. And that is why he took the time to warn them about the dangers that were all around them.

Often, our children get a little frustrated with us as parents for constantly telling them to do this, don't do that, no, you can't go there, etc. They see it as harping on little things, but what they fail to understand is the depth of our love that drives us to make sure they really hear and understand what can hurt them. We love them and do not want them to be hurt. That is why we tell them again and again to be careful and guard against the dangers of this world. If they could understand how much we love them, (and one day when they have children of their own, they will) they would "cut us more slack." We warn them out of love.

Listen to what Paul said in 1 Thessalonians 2:11-12 (NIV), *"For you know that we dealt with each of you as a father deals with his own children, encouraging, comforting and urging you to live lives worthy of God, who calls you into his kingdom and glory.*

There is a story in the Old Testament (1Samuel 2-4) of a high priest, Eli, who had two sons, Hophni and Phinehas. His sons were also priests, but they were wicked. Eli either did not want to know or turned a blind eye to their behavior. He did not warn or restrain them, which is one thing a father does as the high priest of God. Eli should have really done this with both of his sons. As a result of his inaction, all their lives ended tragically. He is an example of how a spiritual father should not act. True love does not ignore sin; it confronts it with a desire to bring the sinner back to God.

We must never abdicate our responsibility, not only to our physical children, but also to our spiritual children. We have a responsibility to keep a vigilant watch over them and to warn them of the dangers that we know are there. We have the experience and knowledge. We have been tripped up a time or two ourselves; and if we know where the potholes in the road are, then we need to make others aware before they hit them.

A Spiritual Father Reproduces Life

"For though ye have ten thousand instructors in Christ, yet have ye not many fathers: for in Christ Jesus I have begotten you through the gospel." (1 Corinthians 4:15 KJV)

Another characteristic of spiritual fatherhood is that spiritual fathers reproduce their life in the lives of others. Paul says, "I became your father through the gospel." The basic definition of a father is that he is a nourisher, protector, sustainer, upholder, progenitor...one who reproduces himself. As Christians, we're called to produce other Christians, aren't we? Now we cannot save them in the sense that we forgive their sins, because we do not have that power, but we can introduce them to One who does forgive their sins, and by that act of leading them to Christ they in turn become Christians and our spiritual children.

Those we bring into the world are those for whom we should also take responsibility for, in terms of their care and nourishment. We read of someone taking his or her child and putting that child in a Dumpster...that is against nature. What parent would do such a thing? No, when parents have children, we should lovingly bring those children home to care for them, nourish them, and take responsibility for them so they don't die. As Christians, we need to do that for those we bring to Christ. We need to take them under our wing and share our very life with them. We want to reproduce people who are like us spiritually. Paul said... *"Keep putting into practice all you learned and received from me—everything you heard from me and saw me doing. Then the God of peace will be with you."* (Phillipians 4:9 NIV)

In order for this to happen, we must share our lives with them and be a living example before them. We must take responsibility for them.

Perhaps one of the reasons why many Christians do not share their lives with others is because they are not living their lives in a way that they would want anyone to share. If that is the case, then the problem needs to be clearly defined and dealt with. We need to live our lives the way Christ wants us to live. Paul says *"Those things, which ye have both learned, and received, and heard, and seen in me, do: and the God of peace shall be with you"* (Phil. 4:9) We need to shape up. We need to get serious about our walk with God and get our lives in order. This is not a game. It is not a casual pastime. What is at stake is the spiritual welfare of others who are depending on us. Just as our own natural children look to us to be their standard as they grow up, so our spiritual children need a standard. By God's grace, you be that standard for them!

A Spiritual Father Sets an Example

"Wherefore I beseech you, be ye followers of me. For this cause have I sent unto you Timothy, who is my beloved son, and faithful in the Lord, who shall bring you into remembrance of my ways which be in Christ" (1 Corinthians 4:16-17a)

This brings us to another example or mark of spiritual fatherhood. A spiritual father sets an example. Paul says, *"Imitate me."* What a powerful statement that is. What does it take to make that kind of a statement? Can we say that to other people?

"Follow me. Follow my example. Imitate me. Do what I do."

A lot of people say, "Do what I say." Sometimes we say that to our children don't we? "Do what I say, not what I do." Kids look at us as if to say, "Who do you think you're kidding?" You see, they don't just hear what we say, they see what we do, and what we do speaks so loud that it overrides what we say. Don't be surprised when they don't follow what we say and begin to imitate what we do.

Live your life as the example that you would want your children to follow in word and in deed and if your life isn't an example, then change it. Change it and make it an example. Paul said that since he could not come, he was sending Timothy. Timothy had been a son to Paul in the faith and by his following Paul as an example, he had learned to live like Paul lived. Paul followed the example of Christ and Timothy knew Paul's lifestyle and teaching so well that he was able to go in Paul's place to share with them how they ought to live. Allow me to say this, it is a great honor when your father trust you enough to go out in his stead. So many times father's long to send their children out on their behalf but due to the fact that they are not being imitators, they end up having to go themselves. That is why Paul said those things that you have seen me do…you do also. They could see Paul's life in Timothy. Timothy had become his spiritual offspring and our children will become like us. Is that not how the kingdom should work? That we become so engrafted in Christ that when people see us they see a direct manifestation of Christ himself.

A Spiritual Father Teaches

"He will remind you of my way of life in Christ Jesus, which agrees with what I teach everywhere in every church." (1 Corinthians 4:17b)

A true spiritual father takes time to teach. He imparts instruction to his children, however the power of the truth which he teaches is reflected within his own life. We need to be consistent. How important that is. We must be consistent not only with what we say—— but also in what we do, because our way of living teaches other how to live. Do an evaluation of your life. Truthfully, I'm shocked sometimes at my own inconsistencies. I have to tell the truth. How about you? Are you ever shocked by your inconsistencies? It should be an encouragement to get it together, because people who do not know Christ are looking to us. So don't live like the devil.

How we behave in church ought to reflect how we behave when no one is looking. There is a quote that says: *"The true character of a man's is not defined by what he does in front of the crowd but instead by what he does when no one is around." ~Unknown*

So if our language changes when we come to church, we need to change our language when we're not in church. If the way we treat people changes when we come to church, we need to change the way we treat people when we're not in church. If the way we treat our children changes when we come to church, you need to change the way we treat our children at home. Husbands, if the way we treat our wife's changes when we come to church, then we need to change the way we treat them at home and the same goes for the wives in regards to how they treat their husbands. We never know when people are looking at us. What are we teaching them? So many times we end up turning people away from the church based upon how we conduct ourselves outside of the House of God. If I had a dollar for every time I heard the excuse that the reason I don't go to church is because of hypocrites ... Boy, I would be a very wealthy man.

We never know who is looking, so we should live consistently.

Live so that it doesn't matter who is looking! Live so that your consistent life teaches others how to live. Remember…God is always looking!

A Spiritual Father Disciplines

"Now some are puffed up, as though I would not come to you. But I will come to you shortly, if the Lord will, and will know, not the speech of them which are puffed up, but the power. For the kingdom of God is not in word, but in power. What will ye? shall I come unto you with a rod, or in love, and in the spirit of meekness?" (1 Corinthians 4:18-21)

A true spiritual father disciplines his children. The Word of God says: *"For whom the Lord loveth he chasteneth, and scourgeth every son whom he receiveth."* (Heb. 12:6) There was a pastor who had a modified version of this passage of scripture on his desk which said "Whom the Lord loves, he beats the hell out of."

In Corinth, some had become arrogant. They were talking big. They were boasting about who they were in God; about what they knew in Christ. They thought they had even surpassed the apostle Paul himself, but Paul says to them, in effect, *"Listen, you guys sure know how to talk the talk, but I'm going to come and see whether you know how to walk the walk! It's one thing to talk. It's another thing to show me that you have got the power to live up to what you say you have and who you say you are."* In other words, "talk is cheap." Paul operated in the power of God. It was not just talk, it was a life with him. Paul said of himself in 1 Corinthians 2:4-5, *"And my speech and my preaching was not with enticing words of man's wisdom, but in demonstration of the Spirit and of power: That your faith should not stand in the wisdom of men, but in the power of God."*

These people were arrogant. They were boastful and Paul said, *"You can say all you want, but when I get there I'm going to see whether you have the power to back it up."*

There's a danger in Christianity that we will just talk the talk. It doesn't take long as a Christian for you to learn the jargon. It is easy to learn how to appear spiritual and we can easily fool people. We can quote the Bible. We can say the right things. We can put on a great show because we learn how to do that. We want to fit in when we're at church. We want to appear as if we're following Jesus, even though we might be living in some kind of sin. So we come to church and put on our church faces. Church should be the kind of place where we can come in our brokenness and in the reality of our situation and be honest about our struggles. If we're going to follow God, then there will inevitably be times of struggle. We are going to have problems. No one said it would be easy? Where does this belief stem from? Not the Bible, for sure.

Perhaps, from some pep rally somewhere, where some "faith" teacher told them that once you accept Jesus all your problems disappear.

Some people can testify that when they committed their lives to God, the real struggles began! Yet, it's a struggle that is worth it. Ultimate victory does not have to wait until after this life is over. We can have that victory NOW! Nobody can take that away from us. The worst the devil can do to us is to kill us, and that only sends us to Heaven. Let's not deceive ourselves by pretending to be something we are not. And let us not fall into the trap of settling for less than God desires to give us. We need to encourage one another to be all that God wants us to be. We even need to admonish and challenge one another if necessary, just as Paul did to the Corinthians.

Discipline ultimately means accountability. It does not mean we have to like it; however, it does mean that we want the results.

The Corinthians needed to be accountable, not only to God, but also to Paul, their spiritual father in the faith. Sometimes we can convince ourselves that God approves of our behavior, when he does not. That is why we need spiritual fathers in our lives and in the church. They help to hold us accountable. They speak correction into our lives. A spiritual father disciplines those he loves, just as our heavenly father disciplines those he loves. It is a mark of fatherhood.

"My son, despise not the chastening of the LORD; neither be weary of his correction: For whom the LORD loveth he correcteth; even as a father the son in whom he delighteth. (Proverbs, 3:11-12)

You see, people see how we live. They see what is really important to us and they follow our example. Do we have the power to back up the talk that we talk? We do in Christ. If we will surrender to him and follow him, he will give us the power to live for him and be the kind of example that we need to be for those that we bring to Christ. Nobody expects us to be perfect, but they do expect us to be real. If we will be real about our struggles and transparent about the problems that we face as we seek to follow Christ with all our heart that will inspire people. Let's live in such a way today that we bring many spiritual children with us.

Chapter 10

The Father's Expectation

"But unto the Son he saith, Thy throne, O God, is forever and ever: a scepter of righteousness is the scepter of thy kingdom. Thou hast loved righteousness, and hated iniquity; therefore, God, even thy God, hath anointed thee with the oil of gladness above thy fellows."
(Hebrews 1:8, 9)

Who are you?

While attending Grambling State University, I was at my pastor's house one day, when my spiritual father (Bennett Smith) was visiting. We discussed ministry and what I felt led to do. I relayed to him how I had preached a sermon while I was back home in California over the holidays. He asked if he could see it, so I went back to my dorm room to get it and took it back to him. As we sat there and watched the tape, he told me to cut it off. My initial thought was that I had said or done something wrong in the sermon, but that was not the case. He began to ask, "Who am I?" Like most others I gave the typical answer; "I am Jesse." He asked the same question again, and again I gave him the same answer. His question of who I am began to challenge me as far as my identity was concerned, because no one had ever asked me who I was.

To say the least, I never did come up with an answer at that time. His next few words after that would greatly affect my level of thinking in regards to my overall identity in Christ. He sat back in the recliner and stated it's been a long time since he saw someone walk and preach with such boldness. He said that one day in his old age while relaxing in his recliner it would be nice to see me preaching the gospel on television. I sat there quietly, considering the possibilities of preaching to a national audience. As our conversation drew to a close, he instructed me to go back to my dormitory, watch my sermon, and pray in tongues. While watching the sermon, I drifted off to sleep not hearing anything. I woke up and repeated the process determined to hear what the Spirit of the Lord wanted to say to me. I fell asleep once again; however, this time was different. In a dream a white sheet dropped down and scriptures were coming at me from every direction. Old Testament scriptures, New Testament scriptures and the one that stood out the most was 1 Timothy 1:3.

"As I besought thee to abide still at Ephesus, when I went into Macedonia, that thou mightest charge some that they teach no other doctrine"

Now this passage of scripture was directed at me at that time and even now, I believe Timothy's life and Paul's expectation of Timothy as a spiritual father to a son is the key thing here. I am not so much concerned with placing emphasis on the passage of scripture that stood out to me. I am; however, interested in pointing out the expectation a father has for his son. This becomes so very vital in today's time because we have so many fatherless homes and as a result we have boys wandering aimlessly, void of any purpose or destiny because they have no father to speak into their lives and tell them what is possible.

<u>The Expectant Father</u>

It is always the Father's Expectation for the son to exceed what he has already done, hence the passage that is used for this chapter. Hebrews 1:8, 9 are the key verses here, but I want us to look at other verses so that we can clearly see the expectation of God the FATHER for His SON, Jesus the Christ. Let us read Hebrews: 1:1-13.

If we pay close attention to what is being done here, we will discover that Christ was and is the fulfillment of the Father's Expectation. It is obvious that there is a transition that is taken place here. Even if you choose not to believe it has taken place at that time, we can clearly see that this is something that is going to happen. While there are numerous verses that can be extracted from this passage of scripture, I just want to emphasize one scripture in particular. Hebrews 1:8 says *"But unto the Son he saith, Thy throne; o God, is forever and ever: a scepter of righteousness is the scepter of thy kingdom."* Do you hear what God the Father is saying to his Son Jesus, "Thy throne, o God." This is the Father calling his Son God, and never once do we read in the scriptures of God referring to anyone else as God. All throughout history we can see how important it is for the fathers to speak into their children's life...particularly the son. Please understand that I am in no way trying to alienate our daughters from this process. I have a ten year old daughter myself and am constantly speaking into her life about her identity, purpose, and destiny in Christ. However, as it relates to sons, we have too many whose fathers have never spoken into their lives, never validated them as men, and never once expressed what was possible for them. Instead, we have had fathers who by reason of their own dreams being crushed, turned around and crushed the very dreams of their children stating and/or wanting to believe that they are training them for the real world.

If we look at the story of David, we discover that David experienced the same trouble with being validated by his father Jesse.

"Again, Jesse made seven of his sons to pass before Samuel. And Samuel said unto Jesse, The LORD hath not chosen these. And Samuel said unto Jesse, Are here all thy children? And he said, There remaineth yet the youngest, and, behold, he keepeth the sheep. And Samuel said unto Jesse, Send and fetch him: for we will not sit down till he come hither. And he sent, and brought him in. Now he was ruddy, and withal of a beautiful countenance, and goodly to look to. And the LORD said, Arise, anoint him: for this is he. Then Samuel took the horn of oil, and anointed him in the midst of his brethren: and the Spirit of the LORD came upon David from that day forward. So Samuel rose up, and went to Ramah..." (1 Samuel 16:10-13)

Here it is that you have a prophet who comes to your house to anoint one of your sons as king and you don't even bring all of them before him. David's father blew him off stating that he was just a shepherd boy; therefore, he saw no need to bring him before Samuel. How discouraging is that to a son's self-worth and self-esteem, to think that your father did not regard you enough to bring you before the man of God as he did his brothers. "David was the eighth son and youngest child of Jesse, his father. He tended sheep while his brothers had seemingly more exciting occupations: they were fighters, but he was only a babysitter for a group of musky, dank sheep. He doesn't seem to be a favorite child of his father, and most of his brothers see him more as an errand boy than a contributing sibling. His father doesn't consider him when Samuel comes looking in his house for a king. His dad brought everybody before the prophet in hopes that one of them might meet with the Lord's approval and end up as king over all of Israel. You know that would have made Jesse famous...the father of a king! That would be a real status builder. Perhaps he himself wasn't sure of his own identity and needed an external boost to elevate himself. Jesse had to put his best foot forward. So, he garnered the support of his sons and brought them all before the prophet...all but one. This one son was not mentioned.

It would have been better for David to have been brought before Samuel and let the prophet refuse him than to have his father ignore him and not allow him the chance to "compete" with the rest of his brothers. It's like Cinderella's wicked stepmother not allowing the young girl to try on the glass slipper when it was clearly made for her. Can you believe it? Everyone was there except for David, who was either ignored or forgotten. I imagine that either ignored or forgotten would present a rock that was hard for him to climb over.

"How does a boy cry for his father to cut holes in the rock when the old man's opinion of him is the very rock that the boy is trying to climb over?"-Bishop T.D Jakes "He-Motions", 2004 pp. 36

One of the hardest struggles of youth is the fear of not having what it takes to make their mark in life. It is a real challenge because they have so much potential, but there are so many obstacles. These obstacles, or rocks, if you will, become harder to cut when they are made out of rejection and set in uncertainty about one's own identity. Many young men succumb to peer pressure not out of weakness, but out of desperation to find some place, group, or person who says, Yes, this is who you are and where you fit. "Even for men who have a sense of who they are, as David surely did from his time alone on the hillside praying and writing poetry as he tended his sheep, we all need validation of that identity." Bishop T.D. Jakes "He-Motion, 2004 pp. 37"

This also reminds me of when Jesus was baptized over in

Matthew 3:17 after Jesus came up out of the water, the heavens open up and we hear the Father, God, saying *"This is my beloved Son, in whom I am well pleased."* What a reassurance that was for Jesus to have God make that publicly known that this is my son AND I am well pleased. How many sons today have longed for their father's reassurance only to be combated with, as Bishop Jakes stated , the rocks of their father's negative opinion. I'm reminded of Chapter 4 in the book of Matthew, where Jesus was led by the Spirit up into the wilderness after his baptism, the Father confirmed who he was. The very first place Satan challenges him after he had fasted for forty days, was the area of his identity "If thou be the Son of God." Had not God confirmed to him and before the public eye that Jesus was his son, I am sure the question of identity that the devil posed would have been a challenge for him. However, since that was not the case, we see Jesus boldly declaring thus says the Lord God to the point where the enemy leaves him for a season. GLORY!!!!

God clearly shows us what the expectation of a father should be for his son, which is for the son to exceed what the father has done, yet always calling to remembrance the legacy that father has left behind. Even if you are one without an earthly father or a father who has abandoned or not played a vital role in your overall development...let me encourage me you...YOU are God's child in whom he is well pleased. This is not predicated on your past, nor based on your future, but simply because he loves you. You're created in his image and God has GREAT EXPECTATIONS for you! Remember, you are a masterpiece because you are a piece of the Master.

Chapter 11

Finding Your Fit

"Now ye are the body of Christ, and members in particular."
1 Cor 12:27

The Body

The word particular used in verse 27 of 1 Corinthians 12 is referred to as "a part do or assigned to." The other meaning it takes on is a "lot or destiny." A member in particular speaks more to something being specific or special instead of something general and broad. When it comes to the body, the Apostle Paul says that the body is made up of many individual parts performing very narrow specialized task.

Our body is made up of many different members who contribute to the whole of the body without trying to do everything in the body. They do very narrow, very specific, very specialized task and they don't get involved with everything else, they do what they are sent to do and that's their contribution to the body as a whole.

So, when the gallbladder is working, the gallbladder is not

interfering with the pancreas, the pancreas is not fussing with the stomach, the stomach doesn't have a problem with the lungs, the lungs have no problem with the heart, because everything is situated to perform one very narrow specific function. So in essence, this make every part of the body important. The scripture says that the ear can't say *"Because I am not the eye, I am not of the body; is it therefore not of the body? If the whole body were an eye, where were the hearing?"*

If the ear said man I wish I was an eye and God granted to the ear the request to be an eye, it wouldn't change it from being an ear...it would just be an ear on the front of your face because God set us in the body as it pleased him. So, he is not going to change your assignment because you're a little confused about where you fit. It is of the utmost importance that we discover what it is God has anointed us to do. This is one of the reasons why controlling and/or territorial attitudes will ruin a body or a business anytime you have a group of people trying to perform a particular task, because a controlling or territorial attitude assumes that their one gift can substitute for many. They assume that their grace can substitute for the graces of many, so they end up starving the body because they are trying supplement for working parts that they have no ability to supplement for and you have people doing stuff they have no business doing. All that simply means is this

NO ONE IS ANOINTED TO MAKE
OTHERS UNNECESSARY .

Of all the anointing, of all the graces, of all the gifting that an individual may have, we do not have the gift of marginalizing our brother or sister. We do not have so much of an anointing that it makes the person sitting next to us unimportant. We do not have so much of a gift that we can be spread abroad like seeds to do everything in the body. We are anointed to perform a very narrow and specialized task. One of the great tragedies of the contemporary church today is that we are attempting to stretch believers beyond God's placement. We are trying to be the "Jack of all trades and the master of none." We are trying to have so many irons in the fire and we place ourselves in a position of spinning plates thus we have people stretching their interest beyond where God placed them. And because we have such broad and diversified investments in things, we are not doing what God has called us to do.

"When you try to do more than you should do, you stop doing what you should do very well, if not altogether"

When we see people trying to go beyond what their calling is or what their purpose is, the problem is that the calling begins to suffer because we can't do everything. I know we have the propensity to think that we are great— and we are—but we're only great within our narrow, specialized assignments. I am sure all of us have a vehicle, had a vehicle, or know someone with a vehicle. Do you know that when we go out to our vehicle and turn it on that there are just some parts in your engine that all they do is turn...from the moment you start your engine to the moment you turn it off...that's all that part does is just keep turning. It would appear to be as the old folk would say a "thankless job." You don't get much recognition in that, but now if that little piece just decides to stop turning, everything in the engine says wait! You call it your car breaking down, but it's the body of your engine saying wait, we have a part that's not contributing and we are not designed to keep going without that part contributing. Do you remember how the Children of Israel as a body stopped functioning because they had a member (Miriam) who was not contributing due to being shut out of the camp for seven days? It is the same principle at work here . So in the church, we experience breakdowns because we have parts that are not contributing to the overall function.

One of the things that happens in the human body is that we have parts that get sick or ill and the part of the body that is sick or ill, affects the whole body. I have gotten up in the middle of the night and hit my pinky toe on the corner of my bedrail and man! That pain shot through my entire body...to the point it felt like it went into my hair and I'm bald. Depending on the severity of the damage, it causes the other parts of the body to now have to supplement for that toe being injured. Here is a question, what do we do when we're injured, hurt and/or have a bruise... we cover it and we cover it until it is healed. So why it is in the church when somebody gets injured or hurt we yank the covers off of them before they are healed. If it's good practice for our physical body, then it ought to be good practice for the church body as well. So if there is a part that falls and/or gets injured, we cover them until they are healed. Bodybuilding, so that every particular part in the body is necessary for the overall successful function, because every part that is not working means a greater weight on the parts that are working and it's taking those parts out of what they should be doing and they are being stretched in order to supplement for that part of the body that is malfunctioning.

"As each part does its own special work, it Helps the other parts grow, so that the whole body is healthy and growing and full of love." Ephesians 4:16 NLT

Know Who You Are Not

We are continuously bombarded with messages on finding

out who you are, well it is just as important to know who you are not. "Ye yourselves bear me witness, that I said, I am not the Christ, but that I am sent before him. He that hath the bride is the bridegroom: but the friend of the bridegroom, which standeth and heareth him, rejoiceth greatly because of the bridegroom's voice: this my joy therefore is fulfilled. He must increase, but I must decrease." John 3: 28

We can clearly see here that John the Baptist fully understands what his part is as it relates to Christ. It's like in a play, everyone is given their parts and there are those who don't like their part, because they desire the leading role. However, what they fail to realize is that the star couldn't be the star and can't shine without it's accompanying and supporting parts. John fully understood this, which is why he emphasizes the truth in stating that he is not the Christ. He says I don't know what you came to see, but I'm not him. I'm here running before him and now that my narrow specialized task is over, I MUST DECREASE. In every body, there is a necessity of our willingness to be able to decrease so that others can increase. Sometimes the light is on your part, but then the light will move somewhere else and you have to be willing and mature enough to recognize that the light has moved on and you decrease while somebody else increases. John knew this, even to the point when Christ came to be baptized of him, John said I have need to be baptized of you and Christ said no...this is your part so in this part I submit to you so we can "Fulfill all righteousness." Can I tell you that your church has been placed by God and you have to learn how to fulfill all righteousness...in other words, you have to learn how to fulfill "your part' as it relates to the body of Christ. Unfortunately, in the contemporary church of today, we have a lot of people who run towards the light and not their position. So when the light moves, they want to move with the light because they are unwilling to humble themselves and allow another to shine. If we are called to fulfill all righteousness—and we are—then it is important for us to know what our particular part is and to know who we are and who we are not.

Get In where You Fit In

When it comes to what you are supposed to do, how do you know what that is? Because you are going to be impacting, successful, you're going to be a benefit to your local body and wherever you go outside of your church by finding out what it is you are supposed to do. One of the things that you will discover is that you are particular about your particular grace. Have you ever seen somebody do something and you said they are sure particular...well they should be as should you be. You are very particular about your particular grace. You are picky in that very picky way about what you are called to do. You are competent to do what you are called to do. If you think you are called to do something that you have no competence for, you're probably not called to do it. In being competent, you will have a certain amount of knowledge about what you are called to do. In that you are competent, brings me to my next point, you are invested. I am amazed at the number of people who say that they are called to do something but you can never get them to do it. You mean to tell me that you are wired, equipped, called, appointed and anointed, authorized and deputized to do a particular assignment and it's hard to get you invested in it. You never had to beg or tell Michael Jordan or LeBron James to practice basketball ball...they are invested. You never had to beg or tell Michael Phelps to practice on his swimming...why? He's invested. You don't have to tell a bird to fly, a fish to swim, a dog to bark, a cat to meow or a cow to moo...why? Because they are invested and it's been engrafted into them that this is what they are called to do. Once an individual finds their grace...their particular grace where God has called them to, you will never have to beg or tell them to do it. They will automatically do it and at that for hours on in, because they are invested.

In addition to finding your grace, you will discover that you get frustrated when you see it done wrong. Let's take someone that is called to cosmetology, don't let them see someone's hair messed up...it drives them crazy. Take a car mechanic in that a very good one, he or she will hate to see a run-down car. Why does this frustrate you? It is because you are invested, particular, and competent about your grace.

Renewable Interest

Whatever you are called or gifted to do, it never gets old. No matter how much you do it or how many times you have to go out and do it—it never gets old. As a matter of fact, you are always coming up with ways to make it more adept to the people you deal with. You never let it get old. Again, I am equally amazed at the people who say that they are getting burned out over what they are created to do. Here is my question...were you ever called to do it in the first place? You may be distracted, you may be confused, you may not understand what your particular assignment is at present but how are you burned out? How are you ready quit and throw in the towel on what you said you were called to do? When you are called to a particular gifting, you will always have a renewable interest.

You will also discover that you have a unique and purposeful understanding of its importance. Anytime you are called to do a thing, you have a very unique perspective about it. In other words, you understand the "why" behind what you do. The

Apostle Paul said in Romans 11:13

"For I speak to you Gentiles, inasmuch as I am the apostle of the Gentiles, I magnify mine office..."

The Apostle was basically saying, I understand the why as to why I am here and I focus on what I am to do and not on what others are doing. Have you ever been to or seen a horse race? They place blinders on the horses so that they are not distracted by who or what's going on in the other lane...they just run their race. Sadly, there are members in the body who constantly get distracted by what's going on in the other lane opposed to running their on race. What they need, if you will, are some spiritual blinders so that they could focus in on the race they have been called to run. What is it that you are called too? Whatever it is be it children's ministry, usher, greeters, parking lot, security etc. whatever it is, you are going to have a unique understanding of the importance of it. There was this pastor of a church and as he came to his office, he saw this little young kid standing outside the door smiling. Interested in knowing what he was so happy about, he asked the little boy "Why are you so happy?" The little boy responded "Have you seen the bathroom yet?" The pastor said "No, I have not been in there yet." Eventually, the pastor went into the bathroom and found it sparkling clean and smelling fresh. He came back out to the little boy and said "Wow, it's spotless and sparkling!" to which the little boy said "see that's my part." The little boy was not trying to be falsely humble; he was saying this is my part, this is my contribution and I'm secure enough in it that I don't have to be intimidated by some who is doing something more noteworthy.

The Thief of Your Grace

"I beseech you therefore, brethren, by the mercies of God, that ye *present your bodies a living sacrifice, holy, acceptable unto God, which is your reasonable service. And be not conformed to this world: but be ye transformed by the renewing of your mind, that ye may prove what is that good, and acceptable, and perfect, will of God. For I say, through the grace given unto me, to every man that is among you, not to think of himself more highly than he ought to think; but to think soberly, according as God hath dealt to every man the measure of faith. For as we have many members in one body, and all members have not the same office:"* Romans 12:1-4

The word office in verse 4 means "service" but also office is the root word for official. I'm sure many of us know the difference between something official and something that's a knock-off. When it comes to something being official, it simply means that the creator or the actual manufacture has placed his hands on it. The knock-off, someone else did it and placed a fake emblem upon it to make it appear real; however, it was not the creator. So when the scripture says that not everyone has the same office, it means that not everyone has been placed by the maker in the same thing. You are official in something in particular...meaning that God has placed his hand on you. Sadly, in the church today, we are seeing a lot of knock-offs and not the real thing. We see a lot of cubic zirconias but not a whole lot of real diamonds, a lot of copies, a lot of patent leather, but not real leather. So there must be an urgency to make sure we are where God has actually placed us. One of the biggest enemies, oppositions and thieves to where God has placed you is thinking "MORE" highly of ourselves than we ought to think. He's not saying that we shouldn't think high of ourselves...but thinking ... *"more highly than he ought to think; but to think soberly, according as God hath dealt to EVERY man the measure of faith"* is where the problem comes in to play. To put it in simple terms, understand that God has placed others here to do other things and you can't do them all.

This scripture in Romans 12:3 is vital because people in today's society don't feel important enough in their place and when you don't feel important enough in your place you will be tempted to move. I'm not getting enough recognition or attention, so let me stretch myself beyond my grace so that I can be seen and when you think of yourself more highly than you ought to think, you are about to do some serious body damage. People who don't feel important enough in their God given assignment, their self-flattering vision of themselves compels them to think they should have something more or better. And, better is normally described as more power, popularity, material prosperity or visibility. It is this sense of wanting to feel more important that causes us to step over the boundaries that God has placed on us. Here is a statement by T.S. Eliot that I believe is apropos to what we are discussing:

"Half the harm that is done in this world is due to people who want to feel important. They don't mean to do harm; but the harm does not interest them. Or they do not see it, or they justify it because they are absorbed in the endless struggle to think well of themselves."

Did you catch the adjective used here "endless struggle?" They are absorbed in the endless struggle to think well of themselves. There is one more quote by Adam Smith that speaks to the same degree which says:

"Examine the records of history, recollect what has happened within the circle of your own experience, consider with attention what has been the conduct of almost all the greatly unfortunate, either in private or public life, whom you may have either read of, or heard of, or remember, and you will find that the misfortunes of by far the greater part of them have arisen from their not knowing when they were well, when it was proper for them to set still and to be contented."

Do exactly what he just suggested...think about it. If you think of all the people who had great misfortunes in life, it was people who did not know when to sit down, shut up and be content. The Apostle Paul speaks to this end when he says over in Philippians 4:11(AMP) "Not that I am implying that I was in any personal want, for I have learned how to be content (satisfied to the point where I am not disturbed or disquieted) in whatever state I am." Are you content with where you have been placed? If not, you will always find yourself in a position thinking that it's all about you.

As It Has Pleased Him

God did not set you in the body as it pleased you; he set you as it pleased him. He placed you as it pleased him and one of the greatest tragedies is that we are not content nor appear to be satisfied with where God has placed us. Every time we step out of our place of grace, calling, gifting we are saying God, I'm not satisfied with where you placed me. Think about this...what would happen if the moon had a will and it up and decided that since I'm not the sun I'm going to move. Do you know how many lives will be lost if this ever happen? So now take into consideration where God has placed you...how many lives are being affected because you up and decide that you don't want to stay where God has placed you.

There was a dictator by the name of Mao Zedong who ruled China during the 1950's era. Needless to say he was given to a lot of self-flattery and had the Chinese people doing god-awful things and is widely believed to have caused the death of roughly 50 million people during his reign. One day he got this idea to launch a campaign against what he considered four pests to the Chinese culture. In 1958 one of Mao's first acts as part of the Great Leap Forward, aimed at eliminating mosquitoes, flies, and rats which made some sense, but rendering them extinct, even locally speaks to his ignorance. The fourth pest, the sparrow, does not seem to belong on this list. But Mao observed that sparrows would eat the grains planted by Chinese workers and, therefore, reduce the value of the people's labor. So they made the list too, and were more effectively targeted than the other three "pests." Mao's government began a large-scale propaganda campaign to get peasants to shoo away or kill sparrows on sight being that the Chinese were grain producing people, he figured that for every million sparrows he killed that 60,000 more people would have grain to eat. So he commanded the Chinese people to keep up loud noises, shoo the sparrows away and kill them if need be. This was their job and if they did not do it, he would take their life. The Chinese people did this successfully until they killed millions of sparrows. So much so, that you could see truckloads of dead sparrows being hauled out from the fields. He thought that if he killed these sparrows, he would have more grain. Well he killed the sparrows not knowing that the sparrow had been placed there by God. You see the sparrow would eat the insects, so when he killed all the sparrows, they had an insect infestation and the locust multiplied into thousands and ate up all the grain. By the time the government realized what was going on, it was too late.

    I cannot stress enough of how important it is to understand purpose and placement. The bumble bee has thousands of little hairs over his body that it uses to pollinate other flowers. If we were to kill all the bumble bees, we would not have any flowers. Sometimes we hold a narrow perspective about things in the body, and we aim to get it, not recognizing the bigger picture and how it would affect the body in the greater scheme of things. Everybody is important to the body, thus He put you where you would have the most value. In Genesis 1 after everything was created you see God saying after each thing He created and placed... "He saw that it was good." Do you know that the gift He has placed in you and where He has placed you in the body is good, meaning that you are a valuable and viable asset to the body? Unfortunately, many people get their value from the world and when where they have been placed doesn't seem to line up with what the world calls valuable, people start trying to move not understanding that they have been placed where they would add the most value, be the most effective, and have the most potential to grow.

Increasing in Value

Your value increases as you add value to other people. The more value you bring to someone else, the more value you gain in your own personal life. Look at Bill Gates, he's added value to people's life by making it available to them to go all around the world from the comforts of their home. You can go to school, work, and church etc. all because of creating the computer. He added value to people's life thus increasing in value himself. Jesus sits as high as you can go...at the right hand of the Father God. He sits so high because he was willing to go so low. The scripture says in Philippians 2:8

"And being found in fashion as a man, he humbled himself, and became obedient unto death, even the death of the cross."

If the body of Christ would catch a hold to this principle the "Law of Humility," we would see a lot more value being added to people's life. That's the Kingdom Principle . Lastly, in Matthew

25:14-28 we discover three men who were given an opportunity to add value to their master.

These three men were all given Talents, to one five (5), to another two (2) and to another one (1) and the scriptures says that the master left on his journey. All but one of the men, specifically the one who received one talent, went out and increased what they were given although we find nowhere in scripture where their master instructed them to go out and do so. However, upon the master's return each of them comes before him with their report of what they did with their talents. The one with five talents says master, you gave me five talents and look; I have gain five more. The master's response is *"well done"*; you have added value to me thus in return I will add value to you by making you ruler over much more. The one with the two talents comes and reports the same thing about his two talents and his master responds to him the same way as he did the one with the five. The servant with the one talents comes and makes an excuse as to why he decided not to add value to the master and bring him what he gave him. What a slap in the face, to do nothing with what you have been entrusted with. It is apparent that the master had confidence in all of them if he entrusted them with talents. Even if it was not all on the same level…they were still given something. How do you view what God has given you? Are you going out and multiplying it or are you just making excuses while sitting on something that was meant to bring value to others.

When we "Find our Fit," and are secure in where we have been placed, it is only then that we will begin to increase others by adding value to them and in turn add value to ourselves.

Chapter 12

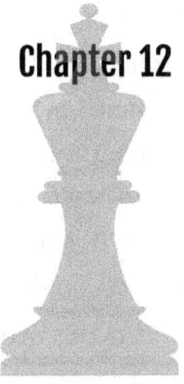

Final Words

As I bring this book to a close, it is my prayer that what has been written herein has a tremendous effect on the lives of those who are called to serve. However, if the truth be known, we are all called to serve whether we realize it or not. If you would, allow me to speak transparently to you as I bring this to a close, I am a firm believer that the Ministry of Help is of great importance to the body of Christ and should not be taken for granted. I am bound by what I teach and preach and do not back down for any reason whatsoever. I have also made some costly mistakes while on this road called the Ministry of Help. Pastors, servants, all of us who are called to serve listen very closely...

"When the ministry that God has given you begins to supersede God himself, you place yourself into a position whereby you no longer have a ministry that serves God and his people but in essence a ministry that you seek to serve you, thus making an idol of that ministry to whose throne you worship.

It is at that point that the ministry is no longer effective because God will not play second fiddle to anything. Additionally, the ministry that God has given you should never place you in a position whereby you view it or yourself as more important than the people it is supposed to serve...thus you have the SERVANT-LEADER. How much more effective do you think the Body of Christ will be when we take on that role. Ministry aid's people, it does not walk over people." -Jesse A. McCrary

Servanthood is costly and if the proper balance is not given to this matter, it may cost you more than what you are willing to pay. I believe that the Ministry of Help is of great importance to the body of Christ and should not be taken for granted, but treated with dignity and respect from all sides. We must, if we are going to be effective in what God has called each and every one of us to do, begin to deal wisely and justly not just in regards to the Ministry of Help, but in all facets of ministry. There are countless number of people whose lives have yet to be touched with the message of the Christ. I believe it is past time for us to come together as one effective and efficient unit to make sure that there are no more, "Casualties of war." Being in a position of servanthood is great and just as Christ has shown us, there is great honor in serving. However, the transition from a servant to a son or daughter is a matter that takes place within the heart whereby we are no longer a servant portraying a son/daughter but a son/daughter who is willing to serve unconditionally. Whether we are in a position of servanthood or a position of sonship, understand that both are very significant to the Body of Christ and there is a reward for all.

Personal Stories from
"The Jordan River Experience"

Adrienne Brown,
Christ Nations Church, Texarkana, Texas
~ Isaac Pitre, Pastor~

"As a member of Christ Nations Church since 2006, I have not only experienced great leadership in Pastor Isaac Pitre but also came to know him as a great spiritual father. I knew he was my spiritual father when I stepped into a time of deception and a spirit of confusion that caused me to act out of my normal character. Most people, even Pastors, would talk about you and not have much to say to you when you make a mistake ... not the case with Pastor Pitre. He continued to show me love and he helped to rebuild me as a person. I never felt that he treated me different, but instead he always loved me...even in my wrong. Of course his Sunday and Wednesday messages always help to keep me on the straight and narrow, but more importantly, his love toward me keeps me wanting to move forward daily. I'm truly thankful for him."

Nikki Lewis,
Christ Nations Church, Texarkana, Texas
~Isaac Pitre, Pastor~

"For as long as I can remember, I have been a church member, but never really understood the term "Spiritual Father" because I had a natural father who was living, it was unnecessary to even delve into that. Since becoming a member of Christ Nations

Church, I have come to the realization that Pastor Isaac Pitre is and will always be my spiritual father. He has taught me like a child of his very own ... his lessons for my life being so simplistic yet so intricately woven into the fabric of my being. Several months ago, he taught on "God's Family" and how much God did to just have a family here on this earth that would represent Him and the Kingdom of God. How

many people he went through, starting with Adam and Eve and how He eventually had to bring back the Perfect Son, Jesus Christ, to be our example. I started to equate some of the points he was using to us, here left to bring the Kingdom of God down to Earth. As members of Christ Nations Church, if we want to represent the King well, there are certain things we don't do, certain places we don't go, and certain ways we are expected to behave ... all with Pastor Pitre as the head of this Family. Maybe without much knowledge, Pastor Pitre has shaped my life, much like a Father would. He has taught me how to live on my own with the Word as my compass, similar to a father who has trained their natural child to face the world of adulthood. He has given me STRONG Word that has left me convicted, headed for repentance and turning away ... also; he has encouraged me in the faith and in several other areas. He has made me aware that my ministry is valid, necessary and has helped me bring it to the people of the church in a Spirit of Excellence. He has walked me right up to the path of my destiny and given me the wisdom to walk worthy in it. I will FOREVER be indebted to my spiritual father, Pastor Isaac Pitre, because he has done so much to train me up in the way I should go and I will NOT depart from it; for in it, is wisdom, destiny, favor, abundant life and blessings I have no room to receive."

Charolett Hollowell,
Christ Nations Church, Texarkana, Texas
~ Isaac Pitre, Pastor~

My family and I first became acquainted with Pastor Isaac Pitre in 1999 during a special 'Miracle Monday' service he attended that was held at our local church at the time. It was the first time we had ever heard of him and heard him minister; there was something different about the ministry that flowed out of him that intrigued us. We made contact with him a few times within that year and the early part of the next. In the summer of 2000.

Pastor Pitre was a guest minister for a mutual friend at his 'Summer Breakthrough Revival' service, it was during the attendance of that service that we realized we were called to him and he to us! From that time, we would get CD's and travel to his church and whenever he was in the area attend those services we could get to. It wasn't until August of 2008 that we moved to Texarkana, Texas and joined Christ Nations Church where Pastor Isaac Pitre serves as senior pastor. For my family Isaac Pitre was spiritual father before he was ever pastor, I can say the benefit of both is quite extraordinary!

Pastor Ezekiel Williams,
The Faith Center, Sunrise, Florida
~Henry Fernandez, Pastor~

I have the great, honor and privilege of experiencing true mentorship from a great Man of God, the man with "Crazy Faith," Bishop Henry Fernandez, Senior Pastor of the Faith Center located in Sunrise, Florida. He has been like an Elijah to me. He took the time to mentor, train, help, encourage, support and develop me in both ministry and even greater in life. He also allows me to see the man behind the "Crazy Faith." It is through spending time with him that I believe I have received of his spirit, and desire to imitate him in ministry and in life. I see how he loves God, his family and people in general. I see his love for life and living his best life now. I see his absolute commitment to being a person of integrity, humility, servant-driven, and to really imitate the person of Jesus Christ. I see his commitment to living a life of love, making excellence the standard for all he does and possessing great faith. I see his unselfish desire to help others reach their full potential and to nullify the prediction and rewrite the future of our youth. I am thankful to God for this tremendous blessing. I reverence the Man of god, because although he is my Bishop, I understand that God is using him to be not only a pastor to me, but more so a spiritual father to me and I do not take that lightly.

I am thankful that he follows the voice of God and not the opinions of people, (because some church-folk can become jealous of you and try to kill a person's character and reputation). I have nothing to really offer him in return, for all he has done for me and how much he has done to help transform my life; except love and loyalty. What would cause someone so great to pick someone so low and offer to help him win in life can only be described as the genuine agape love of God. Some people may misunderstand why I try to do so much in the ministry and may say, "Oh, he's trying to kiss-up and be seen by Bishop Fernandez." Oh how wrong they are. For it brings me great joy to be able to do anything possible to help the Man of God in any possible way after all he has done for me. He is more than just a pastor, boss or mentor, he is my father. And may I live as a spiritual-son, who will bring Glory to God and great honor to my spiritual-father in the Lord, by duplicating in the lives of millions what he so kindly imparted to me.

Minister Danny Davis,
The Faith Center, Sunrise, Florida
-Henry Fernandez, Pastor-

I grew up in the church where my father was an ordained minister (Baptist) and my mother was an organist (COGIC). My parents divorced after 30 years of marriage. I chose to live with my father. My father hated religion but loved the Lord. He knew the Bible front and back so much that other pastors used him as a reference when it came to finding different scriptures. He was like a human "google". My father wasn't a fan of phony people or crooked preachers and he despised ignorance. His prayer of faith came at a very young age, literally during a storm when he was scared of the tornado like winds, thunder and lightning. At that time is when he remembered God promised to take care of him & from that day forward he lived his entire life by faith. Faith also became part of my D.N.A because of my father and his Christian teachings. My father was an educated and hardworking man of integrity. He passed away March 1992. On July 20th my wife and I walked into The Faith Center and for the first time in my life, I felt a connection. Bishop Fernandez taught the word with such clarity and simplicity the way my very own fleshly father taught it. No screaming, moaning or babble. The more I sat under Bishop's teachings, the more my life had begun to change and my understanding had increased. Fast forwarding to January 2012, my wife Erika and I were ordained as ministers. The calling was the start of us walking into our purpose. I especially feel a close connection with Bishop because of our similarities in life such as:

> We are the same age
> Our parents divorced after 30 years of marriage
> Our church upbringing
> Our financial struggles with our wives
> Our sense of humor
> Our faith in God

Our visit to The Faith Center was a divine appointment and Bishop was divinely appointed to be shepherd over our lives. He picked up spiritually where my father left off.

Minister Erika Davis,
The Faith Center, Sunrise, Florida
~Henry Fernandez, Pastor~

I grew up in a very strict Jehovah Witness household. My father was an elder of the congregation which meant he was like the pastor. My mother was a regular pioneer which meant she had to put over 100 hours per month into the ministry. In other words, she had to spend a lot of time going "door to door" speaking about the "Kingdom of God." By the age of 18, I decided that I no longer wanted to follow in my parent's footsteps and married out of "the will of God" or so they told me. Danny was the total opposite of what I was programmed to marry. He was a preacher's son, 10 years older than I was and had a son. 3 strikes! Danny and I went through serious issues in our marriage. Once we decided to quit playing and get right with God, we attended the Faith Center together. That very Sunday, Bishop Fernandez was teaching on "Success in your Marriage, Family and Finance." From that point forward, our marriage became stronger than ever. Once we decided to get serious with God, my entire family turned their backs on me. They labeled me an apostate and have totally alienated me from the entire family including nieces, nephews and brothers. I have drawn closer to Bishop and looked at him as my spiritual father and somewhat of an earthly father because mine is currently not in my life. Bishop has prayed for me during the darkest hours and has helped me stay grounded in the word, assuring me that the situation with my family will be my greatest testimony if I just hold on!

Minister Phil Lake,
The Faith Center, Sunrise, Florida
~Henry Fernandez, Pastor~

I've been a member of the Faith Center Ministries for about 14 years and the thing that attracted me the most was the word being preached. As my spiritual father, Bishop Fernandez has a unique way of making the word practical....and his life reflected the same things. It's one thing to hear about faith or to even think you're walking in it, but it's another thing to see faith manifested in the natural. I would say that's when I saw Bishop Fernandez as a father figure. His walk of faith in every area of his life even in the birth of his two sons was just amazing to me. Those examples along with many more have increased my faith walk with the Lord. It's like the Elijah Elisha example. I'm close to Bishop, so to not walk in the same faith or higher says a lot about my relationship with God, so I'm determined to take the word literally concerning every area of my life. If God can do it for my leader then surely He can do it for me because He has already promised us blessings, favor and great health.

Judge Ilona Holmes
The Faith Center, Sunrise, Florida
~Henry Fernandez, Pastor~
From Pastor to Father

I met Pastor Henry Fernandez in November 1995. I had heard a lot about his church growth. My curiosity led to my visit, which never ended. When I arrived at the church, I gave my business card to an usher and asked her to give it to the pastor. The church was packed, so I was seated Closer to the back of the church (learned a valuable lesson to get to church on time). I have to candidly admit that I was a bit uncomfortable in a church named Plantation Worship Center (we were in Lauderhill and not Plantation), but the people were warm and friendly.

I started enjoying the good music and singing. Then I saw this little man walk up the stairs to the pulpit. I figured that he was in his late twenties or early thirties. Then all of a sudden I heard him calling my name and asking me to come to the pulpit. He handed me a microphone and asked me to introduce myself to the congregation. I was impressed and I liked him mainly because of his friendly smile. After the introductions I settled into my seat and waited for the sermon. I know preachers and preaching and I didn't think that this young man would know much. Boy, was I wrong. Not only was he young, friendly and charismatic, he preached like a mad man. Powerful, potent and faith filled. I continued to "visit" the church (I was a tithing member and faithful, I forgot to officially join). I became the Pastoral Care Director in 1997 and remain in that capacity today. It was when I accepted this position that I began to feel more than a member and more like a daughter. My job description is to take care of Bishop and his family but I think they take care of me.

Even though he wasn't a biological father, yet, Bishop Henry Fernandez had all the attributes of a father. He is patient, humorous, thoughtful, humble and wise beyond his years. However, I have seen the serious, stern, no nonsense side of this man when it comes to ministry. My father died when I was 15 years old. My mother never remarried so I didn't have a man that I thought of as a "father figure" until now. Even though I am five years older than he is, Bishop always looks out for me to make sure all is well. He checks on me when I travel out of town. He checks on me when I'm in very stressful trials. I feel that I can talk to him about anything. When I'm about to "go off" my phone will often ring and it's him checking on me. Even now, after a long wait of 16 years before he became a biological father, he still has that fatherly aura when it comes to me. I love and respect him as my pastor and spiritual leader and as my father. He is a blessing from God.

Pastor Brad Jacquett
The Faith Center, Sunrise, Florida
~Henry Fernandez, Pastor~
Bishop as a spiritual father

I came to the Faith Center with my family in Passover of 199[?] This was one of the best and most profound decisions that we hav[e] made that we totally believe that this was the perfect will of God. Serving as a minister in my first church and also being raised fro[m] a child as a preacher's kid I knew the importance of having a goo[d] spiritual leader who is grounded in the word of God.

God is amazing in the way he does things. I never ever trie[d] to mention dreams I had because of the way many Christians g[et] so mislead and taken up into dreams in a negative way; howeve[r] I found this dream as awesome and divine when I realized that [it] involved Bishop Fernandez. This was at the same time that we we[re] praying for direction for a new church home. I dreamed that I too[k] my family on a journey where we walked through a wilderness an[d] came to a place that was like a district under the earth. We were n[ot] welcomed by an individual there although we had asked directio[n] from a woman who tried to help us, immediately we were drive[n] from there by her husband. Shortly after we found ourselves on to[p] of a mountain a beautiful place where we met a young man nea[t]ly dressed who smiled at us and said "Let me show you the way[."] When I came the first time to The Plantation Worship Center I sa[w] Bishop Fernandez I said to my wife " that is the young man I saw i[n] my dream". It was an immediate confirmation that he was the perso[n] to be our spiritual father and leader. After much prayer and oth[er] confirmations, we were certain he was the one God wanted to be ou[r] spiritual father.

94 I've found Bishop Fernandez and Pastor Carol as two peop[le]

that have the heart of Christ, genuine, real and love God and his people with a special love like none other. Bishop preaches and teaches just the way Jesus does it, he said only what the Heavenly Father tells him what to say. He is not the type to leave the sheep but lead, love and guide them just like Jesus. Thank God for a man of God like Bishop Fernandez who has a heart of gold, loving his family his children both natural and spiritual. I love and admire Bishop Fernandez as my father in the Gospel, he believes in us and is so patient with us even when we as his children are not loving, genuine or consistent. This is the true attribute of a real spiritual father and my family and I love him very much. We do not have many fathers in Christendom like that. God bless Bishop Fernandez.

About the Author

JESSE A. MCCRARY is founder of the F.A.T.H.E.R ME Initiative. He is a motivational speaker, leadership development trainer, author and teacher. Having traveled nationally and internationally, his practical approach to the scriptures has opened the eyes of many by helping them to see the plan and purpose of God in their lives. He addresses critical issues affecting youth and young adult today as it relates to their social and spiritual development. The central theme of his message is restoration by way of reconciliation and maximizing the individuals God given abilities. Jesse, along with his daughter Charis Alethia reside in Florida and are members of The Faith Center under the teachings of Bishop Henry and Pastor Carol Fernandez.

www.ingramcontent.com/pod-product-compliance
Lightning Source LLC
Chambersburg PA
CBHW052111110526
44592CB00013B/1560